Women of Coal

Women of Coal

RANDALL NORRIS

JEAN-PHILIPPE CYPRÈS

WITH INTRODUCTIONS BY

DENISE GIARDINA   NIKKI GIOVANNI
JIM WAYNE MILLER   HELEN LEWIS

THE UNIVERSITY PRESS OF KENTUCKY

Editorial and Sales Offices: The University Press of Kentucky
663 South Limestone Street, Lexington, Kentucky 40508-4008

96 97 98 99 00   5 4 3 2 1

Library of Congress Cataloging-in-Publication Data

Norris, Randall, 1949-
    Women of coal / Randall, Jean-Philippe Cyprès ; with
introductions by Denise Giardina . . . [et al.].
        p.   cm.
    ISBN 0-8131-1993-6
    1. Women coal miners—Appalachian Region—Interviews.
2. Coal miners' spouses—Appalachian Region—Interviews.
3. Children of coal miners—Appalachian Region—Interviews.
I. Cyprès, Jean-Philippe, 1959-   II. Title.
HD6073.M6152U66   1966
305.4'2'0974—dc20   96-33249

*We would like to dedicate this book
to the women of coal,
whose recollections of the past,
struggles in the present, and
visions for the future
make their lives meaningful
and this book possible.*

CONTENTS

continued

PREFACE

While I was growing up, my father was disabled and my mother worked as a secretary to support our family. I learned early on that mountain women are the backbone and strength of their families and communities. I also learned that these women rarely have an opportunity to speak out and tell the world about their hopes, dreams, fears, aspirations, what parts of their culture they would like to keep, and what parts they would like to change. Fundamentally, this book is about "speaking out," hearing voices that otherwise might not be heard, and looking at the images of the speakers as they tell us things we all need to know.

During the past three years, Jean-Philippe and I have traveled extensively throughout the central Appalachian coalfields, sharing women's lives, taking their pictures, and listening to their stories. Whenever someone asked us what kind of women we were looking for, we always said, "Strong women with strong stories." We were never disappointed. As the book evolved, we learned that women in the mountains are not oppressed; they lead happy, exciting lives centered around their families, their careers, and their communities. We also discovered that after one hundred years of exploitation and domination by the coal industry, the infrastructure in many communities is being rebuilt from the ground up, and the women in this book, as well as countless others, are doing the building. It is a Herculean task, but the strength, courage, honesty, and integrity that they have exhibited in the face of this rebuilding is remarkable.

Putting this book together was not an easy task. We spent countless hours driving, talking, typing, working in the darkroom, and figuring out ways to pay for our trips. Each vignette was reconstructed from a forty-five-minute taped interview. Whenever possible, each woman read and validated the narrative, checking factual accuracy; all changes suggested were incorporated into the text. The one thing that spurred us on throughout the process was our belief that the stories of these women need to be told; they are gripping narratives and visual proof of lives lived, lost, and ongoing that are both compelling and dramatic. Wanting to share that human drama with the reader is what kept us going, and now we both feel that we have accomplished our goals—I have brought you their voices and stories, as honestly as I could, and Jean-Philippe has served as "faithful witness" to what he has observed.

Jean-Philippe and I would like to take this opportunity to thank our wives and children, as well as our close friends, for putting up with what goes into making a book. We would also like to thank Virginia Smith for having the vision to see *Women of Coal* as a book; our contributing authors, Denise Giardina, Nikki Giovanni, Jim Wayne Miller, and Helen Lewis, whose interpretive essays add depth and texture to the book; and a special thanks to Jim Wayne, whose technical and editorial help were essential. We would also like to thank the Kentucky Humanities Council and the Kentucky Oral History Society for their generous financial support, without which this book would never have been completed.

PART ONE

COALFIELD WOMEN

In 1965, Ollie Combs watched as strip miners destroyed the mountain behind her eastern Kentucky home. Although she owned the land, she had not given her permission to strip-mine it. In Kentucky at that time, the coal company did not need the landowner's consent.

So Granny Combs laid down in the front of the bulldozer and refused to move until deputy sheriffs came and carried her off to jail. She became the Rosa Parks of the movement against strip-mining in Appalachia, a movement that today is floundering in the face of governmental indifference and animosity but in the late sixties and early seventies came oh so close to securing a total ban on stripping. Twenty years later a spiritual descendent of Granny Combs, sixty-five-year-old Elizabeth Wooten, stood in the rotunda of the Kentucky state capitol in Frankfort, squinted into the bright lights of TV cameras, and vowed to keep her land from being strip-mined without her permission. She would go to court, she said, and if that failed, she would block the bulldozers with her body as Granny Combs had done. Elizabeth Wooten never had to place her body in front of a bulldozer. Thanks to her efforts and those of many other Kentucky women, a statewide referendum banning strip-mining without permission passed with 82 percent of the popular vote in 1988.

Ollie Combs and Elizabeth Wooten are just two of many, many strong Appalachian women of their generation who faced up to the exploitation of the coal industry. Others formed the backbone of the War on Poverty of the 1960s, fought as it should have been fought—by local people on their own turf. These women, often themselves lacking adequate health care or education, set up health clinics and Head Start programs, spearheaded organizing efforts for welfare rights, and were in the front lines of the grassroots labor movements of the era.

But the women of that generation were themselves heirs to a rich tradition of protest extending all the way back to the women who endured incredible hardships in the early coal camps. From the late nineteenth century through the early twentieth, women lived through the loss of the family farm, watched their young sons go into the mines, lost entire generations of men to underground explosions, struggled to feed and clothe a family on an inadequate income, and carried this struggle into tent colonies where they faced starvation, cold weather, and disease.

This pioneer generation of women of coal trod the picket line along with their men. Mother Jones, the legendary labor organizer, describes a strike in which women gathered at a mine and with hoes, shovels, and even a frying pan, attacked "scabs" who had crossed the picket line. Their daughters and granddaughters did the same, walking picket lines throughout the bloody 1930s and the roving picket days of the 1960s and sitting in front of coal trucks in accordance with the nonviolent tactics of strikes in the 1980s. The fight is not over. A new generation of women continues on, and their lives are celebrated in this volume. Their lives reflect to some extent the changes in the coalfields. The classic labor confrontations have subsided for the time being (though hardly permanently) as the United Mine Workers of America (UMWA) seeks to deal with the national realities of the 1990s. In the face of overwhelming external forces that have put horrific pressure on coalfield economies, the greatest challenges have become the preservation of community and the fight to hold onto standards of living.

Anyone old enough to recall life in the coalfields during the 1940s through the 1960s can remember a time of vibrant towns filled with stores and movie theaters, places with a cultural life that included live concerts, dance and music lessons, youth recreation programs, active civic organizations, a variety of restaurants, and efficient public transportation systems. All this is long gone. And although coal companies once provided such basic services as water, sewage, and heating, the systems that provided for these necessities of life have also deteriorated.

Coalfield women have stepped into this very large gap, and this volume celebrates their achievements. Here we meet women who are providing leadership in community life, environmental advocacy, labor organizing, health care—a dazzling array of activities. Women like Cosby Totten, a Virginia coal miner who was one of the leaders of the stirring UMWA strike against the Pittston Company. Singer, songwriter, and organizer Elaine Purkey, who has drawn praise from such greats as Pete Seeger. Nannie Spencer, an evangelist in my native McDowell County, West Virginia. And Addie Davis, working to bring jobs to that same economically hard-hit county. These and scores of other women share their lives in these pages. They are young and old, black and white, housewives and community activists, and coal miners and schoolteachers. They destroy the stereotypes of Appalachian women that have persisted for far too long. And most important, they demonstrate that when the survival of the community is at stake, women are in the forefront of the fight for survival.

Denise Giardina
Charleston, West Virginia

> *My daddy was a miner. My brother was a miner. My husband,*
> *Elmer, was a miner. My sister's children are miners.*
> *Luke, my husband now, was a miner.*

In 1923, Momma and Daddy moved from a farm in Ben Hur, Virginia, to Inman, Virginia, so daddy could work in the mines. He was twenty. He worked awfully hard. He'd come in so tired he'd pull his dirty coveralls off and lay on the floor in his old, ragged pants. He couldn't afford underwear. Nobody could. The next morning he'd pull his overalls back on, grab his lunch bucket, and go back to work. When Hoover was President, Daddy worked for $1.92 a day. Sometimes we had something to eat, and sometimes we didn't. We nearly starved to death. After Roosevelt got in, wages got better, but times were still hard.

I remember wading snow to Linden's Store, with a note Momma had sent for two dollars' worth of scrip. I'd tell the woman in the store I wanted two dollars' worth, and she'd only give me a dollar. Then I got smart. The next time I told her I wanted three dollars' worth, and she gave me two. It was a long walk, and my shoes had big holes in them. I put pasteboard over the holes, but by the time I got back home my feet were so frozen Momma had to put them in a dishpan of warm water just to thaw them out. Back then you didn't have money to buy shoes. I guess that's the reason I like shoes so much today, because I didn't have any then.

In 1940, when I was sixteen, I got married. I worked at home. I milked cows, raised hogs, and planted a garden. I raised four children and a neighbor boy. Since I got married so young, I grew up with the kids. We played football and pitched horseshoes. The kids didn't do without much. All of them graduated from high school, and one of them graduated from college.

Elmer worked at Virginia Iron and Coal. He retired sixteen years ago after thirty-three years in the mines because he had black lung and a weak heart. He just drew forty-five dollars a week compensation, so I had to go to work to help pay the bills. I worked eight years at the hospital. Three years ago Elmer died. We were married forty-eight years, and I can't remember a time when the mines weren't a part of my life.

My oldest son, Jerry, still works in the mines. He runs a machine that cuts coal at the face of the mine. When they brought in all that machinery, it took away a lot of jobs, but the jobs that are left are good ones. I don't see the jobs in the mines disappearing. I think things will stay just about the same. There will always be some jobs in the mines.

Ruth Bush Anderson
Woman of coal
Big Stone Gap, Virginia

From my mother, my grandmother, my family members, and other women I've known, I've learned that mountain women carry the family, and the family revolves around them.

When I moved back home to Harlan County, I wanted to do something to address two or three major issues. I wanted to tell stories that would help children learn how to read, and I wanted to highlight some of the problems around here, like stereotyping and littering. I finally hit on storytelling as the ideal way to get my points across, because I've learned that if children are having fun, they can remember anything.

I started telling stories at the Youth Center in Harlan. When I walked into the storytelling room, I introduced myself as Granny Gail and that worked real well, because I'd come in wearing jeans and tennis shoes and a work shirt, with my hair pulled back. I didn't look like a granny, and the kids picked up on that immediately. I used my appearance to show them that things aren't always the way they think they are, and I used the Jack tales to get my other points across.

I told them about the mean guys who took Jack's tablecloth, and when one of the kids asked me why they were so mean to Jack, I said I didn't know, but maybe they'd been drinking, and when someone drinks they get real mean. I pointed out that Jack didn't drink because he took care of things, so it was a good idea not to drink a lot. Later, I started a storytelling hour at the local schools, and I knew that someday I wanted to work there and help the kids. I'm well on my way now.

I'm going to Union College this fall to get my teaching degree. I'm going to teach history in elementary and junior high school. I'm going to stay in the mountains and work with mountain children, and I'm going to teach them they have a future because they have a fantastic heritage, just like I do. I'm part Cherokee, and I'm very active in Native American affairs; I'm the chief of the Otter Band, Southeastern Cherokee Confederacy, and I'm also chairperson of the Repatriation Committee, as well as being on the Board of Trustees for Sacred Tribal Grounds.

I feel like I'm a traditional mountain woman. Grandma taught me to quilt, to sew, to cross-stitch, to crochet, to bleach honeysuckle and weave baskets out of it. She taught me to plant a garden and to take care of chickens. I still do all those things, but at the same time I use that knowledge about the past to help me in my daily life and to help build a future for myself and my family.

My daughter's twenty-eight, and she was so encouraged when I went back to school that she joined the nursing program at Corbin Baptist Hospital. She's ready to start her clinicals this fall at St. Mary's, and she's got a bright future ahead of her, just like my granddaughter, Jessie. I want Jessie to understand that she has the strength of a mountain woman, and that gives her the ability to go anywhere in this world and be anything she wants to be.

Lindia Gaile Fee
Chief and storyteller
Otter Band Cherokee
Loyall, Kentucky

After I received a B.A. in communications at Virginia Tech, I married and moved to Grundy. My first job was as an aide in Chapter I reading at Vansant Elementary. A few months later, I started teaching preschool in a program called Even Start, where parents who didn't have high school diplomas took GED classes while their children were being taken care of in the same building. I worked with the preschool children, from birth to kindergarten. I chose the two- and three-year-olds because I decided if I was going to teach someone, I wanted to be the first one to get ahold of them. It was a wonderful program, but after a year and a half we had a reduction in force (RIF), and since I was the new teacher, I was let go.

I hated losing my job, but it turned out to be a blessing in disguise. I got to stay at home with my first child until I started working at the library. I love working with kids. Kids are the same everywhere. Children don't have prejudices or biases until later on in life. They're very honest and open, and pure of mind. I also like their sense of wonder and amazement. Since no one has told them not to dislike something, they enjoy doing things and they're willing to try anything.

Like me, most of the women who have come into the area have married someone from here. I think most of them have done all right. It depends on the individual. I'm the kind of person who believes that nobody is going to make you happy but yourself. Your husband's not going to make you happy, your children aren't going to make you happy, you make yourself happy. Just recently, when Stan Parris came here for his trial sermon at Vansant Baptist Church, that's what I told his wife, Susan. I told her that her husband had just preached on making your own happiness, and if she moved here, that's what she'd have to do. I told her Grundy was a wonderful place to live, but it was up to her what she made of it. It's a lot different here than it was in Atlanta, where I grew up. People here in Grundy really care about each other. I found that out when I married. They gave me a wedding shower fit for a queen. I bet I sent 250 thank-you notes! Wedding and baby showers here are really special. They really celebrate them! Probably because the family unit is so strong.

The only drawback to living in Grundy is that you have to go somewhere else to get specialized services. It takes over an hour to drive to Abingdon, two hours to get to Bristol, and seven hours to get to Richmond. That makes it difficult when you're pregnant. Although Buchannon General Hospital has a state-of-the-art cancer center, it doesn't have an OB/GYN doctor on staff, so when you have a baby you have to go to Richlands, Pikeville, Bluefield, or Abingdon. Both my children were born in Abingdon, and I take them back to the doctor who delivered them. Transportation can be a problem in the mountains, but for me it's a minor issue, because I love it here.

Angie Mutter
Children's story hour
Buchannon Public Library
Grundy, Virginia

> *No one tells our children that life is a bed of roses; they're going to have hard times, and they're going to get disgusted and discouraged, but they've got to keep trying.*

Growing up in Welch was like living in one big, happy family. My parents were both schoolteachers; my mother taught elementary school until I was born, and my father taught at Welch-Dunbar Junior High School. I was surrounded by aunts, uncles, and cousins. My parents came here at an early age. They grew up here; they taught a lot of the younger people. The family was well respected and everybody knew us.

Back then we went to segregated schools, but the black schools were tough; students had to perform, because if they didn't, the principal called Momma, and then you were in trouble! My father bought a set of encyclopedias before we even started school, and the first thing I learned to read was the headlines of the *Welch Daily News.* I was the salutatorian in ninth grade. The next year, I had to ride the bus seven miles to Kimball High School. There were times when I thought about riding a bus seven miles when there was a school right here in Welch, but I never worried about it, because I got a good education.

I met Ray, my husband, when we were both high school sophomores. When we graduated from high school we both attended Bluefield State College. After he was drafted into the army we were married November 30, 1943. I remained in college and received my bachelor's degree in education. When he was honorably discharged from the army, Ray returned to Bluefield State College and graduated cum laude with a bachelor's degree in education. He later received his master's degree from West Virginia University in Morgantown and his certificate of graduate studies from Virgina Polytechnic University in Blacksburg.

We raised seven children, all of whom have college degrees. However, after they received their degrees they were forced to move elsewhere to find employment. That's when I realized that there are no jobs here for young, black, educated people.

Our middle son began attending an integrated school in third grade. His new principal, a white woman, was a victim of her own prejudice. She placed him in the lowest group, with the slow learners and the retarded students. We asked for a conference with her, after which he was placed in a higher group. Later, one of his high school teachers, who was also a white lady, discovered he had a reading problem and worked with him to correct it. He graduated with honors from the University of Tampa. Today, he works at Johns Hopkins University and is pursuing his doctorate degree.

Many black people who had college degrees worked in the coal mines. When the mines closed, they lost their jobs. When integration came, most of the African American schools were absorbed into the white schools, and that took away even more jobs. When that happened, just about everybody in the black community left; those who stayed are mostly retired.

Christine Williams
Retired social worker
Welch, West Virginia

I recently asked one of my friends why it took her so long to get involved, and she said she wanted to wait and see if I could do it and live to tell about it.

I got involved in this environmental fight because I lived next door to National Electric Coil Company in Dayhoit, Kentucky. They're a mining machine repair shop that uses cancer-causing degreasing solvents. We all thought National, which was owned by Cooper Industries in Houston, Texas, was closely monitored by the Environmental Protection Agency, but in 1989, when the EPA came to Dayhoit and shut down all our wells, we discovered we were wrong. National had never had a state or federal permit to either use or dispose of chemicals. Whenever they finished a job, they just dumped the chemicals into the Cumberland River.

When the EPA showed up, they told us not to drink the water, wash our cars, water our gardens with it, or take a bath in it. They also told us everything would be fine, but they lied. Last year, four people in Dayhoit died from cancer, and many others have cancer. Even now, three years later, seventy-five families are still drinking water from contaminated wells.

At first, when we started the Dayhoit Citizens Group, we were very naive. We thought this was a problem that could be "cleaned up" like you'd clean up a house. We also wanted the state and federal government to help us determine the extent of our health problems, and we wanted a trust fund set up to monitor our health. Later, we learned there was no "cleanup" for Dayhoit, because there was no "solution" available, and the best idea they could come up with was to reverse the aquifer, which would take forty or fifty years.

That was when we began to encourage people to get involved, because we knew we'd been victims of a real social injustice. This had been done to us because we were poor people. McGraw-Edison ran a similar plant in Louisville, and it was legally permitted. What was done in Dayhoit was criminal. Cooper Industries weighed the costs, and they decided it was cheaper to poison people.

Fighting them hasn't been easy. I've been run off the road, my phone's been tapped, and my job as a teachers' assistant disappeared. All these things made me angry, but I haven't given up. I continue to work within the system, because I don't want to lower myself to their level, and I think it has finally paid off; we've been added to the Superfund list, and now I think more and more women will take an active role, because they're beginning to realize, like I did, how a lot of things going on around us affect our families. If I can get one of them to speak out, to me that's a victory.

Joan Robinett
Environmental activist
Dayhoit, Kentucky

My mother got married just after World War I, when she was sixteen or seventeen. At the time, she was writing scrip for U.S. Steel in the Gary District, and after she got married, she and Dad moved all through the coalfields. Dad worked in mines where he used mules and he shot his own coal. I know at one time when mother was pregnant, she went in the mine with him late at night and twisted the newspapers so he could shoot the coal. The next day he went back in and hand-loaded the coal. They moved from Glen Alum to Coalwood and lived there for sixty-five years.

My childhood was wonderful. Coalwood had its own doctor, dentist, library, drugstore, churches, newspaper, motion picture theater, tennis courts, swimming pool, and a company store where you could buy anything. The company store was not a rip-off. It may have been prior to the UMWA, but during my childhood it was not. I went to elementary school and junior high school in Coalwood, but we had to go seven or eight miles to War to finish high school, where I graduated in 1958. I got married right after graduation.

I began working in the public school system in 1964. At first, I was a secretary. I did transcripts, typing, and filing. But after McDowell County started free kindergarten classes, I became an aide for early childhood education. I loved it. I stayed for sixteen years, and while I was there I took a few classes in psychology and math. I usually worked in a government-funded remedial reading center. Some of the children needed someone to sit down and work with them one on one, because a lot of their parents didn't know phonics.

My husband started out as a rodman working for the engineers, but he wanted to make more money, so he went into the mines. He was inside the mines for twenty-eight years as a section foreman, and when he came out he went into their training program and retired after thirty-five years with the same company. We had three daughters, and they say they just loved the way they grew up in comparison to cousins who lived in Chattanooga and Richmond and other places. We always managed to take the children on vacation every year. We still have a family reunion at Daytona Beach, with my brother and his family. All three of my daughters are married, and we have six grandchildren and they're all straight A students.

I wouldn't change anything about my childhood or my adulthood. I don't think many people, even my grandchildren, have had as calm and as good a life as I've had in the coalfields. I don't regret any of it, and I've never been ashamed of any of it. I'll stand up and fight anyone that puts it down.

Virginia E. Beavers
Head Start aide
Coalwood, West Virginia

My mother's first husband, my Dad's brother, and my first cousin were all killed in the mines. Dad was a coal miner, and while he was at work, Mom spent the whole day worrying about whether or not he was going to come home. That was pretty rough on them, because back then, there were lots of mine explosions. In '57 Bishop blew up twice; it killed thirty-nine the first time, and twenty-seven the next time. In '58 Amonate blew up, and twenty-two men got killed. From the time I was a child, somebody was always getting killed or crippled. I was going to funerals when I wasn't really old enough to know what they were. I didn't want to go into the mines at all.

Before I went to work in the coal mines, I was making minimum wage, $2.30 an hour, and I couldn't raise six kids or operate a vehicle on minimum wage. In the mines I made forty-nine dollars a day. That was big bucks when I started, but when I got laid off six years later, I was making just under eighty dollars a day. That's basically what coal mining meant to me. It was a way to raise my kids until they were old enough to get out of school. I was numb my first day on the job. I didn't know what to expect, but I walked in and shoveled the belt all day. Some of the other miners tried to help me because I was a woman, but I wouldn't let them. I knew if I wanted to be a coal miner the only way I was going to learn how was by jumping in there and doing it. After I got the hang of it, I started to like it, particularly after I joined the union. I already knew what the union was.

When I was growing up and Dad was on strike, we'd all sit around the dinner table, and Dad would ask us what we thought. He'd let us have our say, then he'd explain the way he felt. By the end of the meal, we saw it just the way he did. He was a pretty smart educator. Because of him, I knew what the union meant, and I knew it was good for me, no matter what anybody said. I also knew not to ever cross a picket line, no matter what.

I worked in the mines until I was permanently laid off in October of 1982. I decided I wasn't going to plan my life around being called back to work, so I got involved in other things. I was accepted into the Southern Appalachian Leadership Training program, and that lasted nine months. I learned how to work on issues. I was interested in parental leave, and I still am. I also worked with the Coal Employment Project, and one of our main goals was to get other groups around the country to take on parental leave as an issue. I think we did it. Someday, it's going to be a law.

If I could see into the future, I probably wouldn't look. I don't want to see tomorrow until tomorrow comes. I'm willing to wait, because the future doesn't look too good for working people. This system should have a way to earn a living built into it. Work gives people their dignity, and in the United States, you're not worth anything unless you're drawing a paycheck.

Cosby Ann Totten
Coal miner
Tazewell, Virginia

When Roy proposed, he said, "I want to be your arms."

In 1961, I graduated from high school, and I was planning on starting cosmetology school in the fall. But by the time school started, I became ill with dermotomyocytis. It's a combination muscular and skin disease and, like muscular dystrophy, it makes the muscles very weak. At the time, they didn't know very much about it, because it was very rare; they just knew it was usually fatal. In the fall, I'd gotten down to 113 pounds, and I started getting very weak; when I'd bend over my muscles would tighten up, and I finally reached the point when I got down I couldn't get up. By April 1962, I was in a wheelchair, and they told me I would only live two more years, but I found out the Lord had other plans.

My doctors were amazed. I was in the hospital seven months, and even though my treatment required medications that were very depressive, I never became depressed. I knew my family was already going through a battle, having to deal with my disease and with my being in the hospital, so they didn't need any more problems. After I came home, they gave me shots and turned me over at night, because I couldn't even turn over in the bed. Their special love and their support kept me going.

I met Roy at the Woodrow Wilson Rehabilitation Center in Arlington, Virginia. He'd had his back broken in a rock fall. We were at the center for about a year. He was taking training in upholstery, and I was taking business management. I didn't like him at first. In fact, I tried to get away from him. Later, I came here and stayed with his mother for a year and a half. She's a marvelous, special lady. I stayed with her until Roy and I could get our house built. It was a different kind of courtship, and it was a different type of love and support that I shared with him. It made me want to do more on my own. Three years after I met Roy, I made my own wedding dress, and we got married.

Back then, it was hard to get around. There weren't many places to go, and those few where we could go weren't accessible. When we went somewhere we couldn't stay long, because we couldn't get into the bathrooms. Also, neither of us drove. I'm very fortunate. Three ladies from church take me anywhere I need to go. The new handicap laws have definitely made things better for me and for other people who have handicaps. Now, when I go to town or even out of town, there are places with bathrooms and ramps. But it isn't just the physical things that can slow you down. I've known people up on their feet who don't know how to live.

We've been married for twenty-three years, and every day we try to treat each other like it's our last day together. We enjoy each day, because today is all we've got. I think when a person comes to that place, when they can treat everybody like it's their only opportunity to share love with them, to share the Lord with them, to share the wonderful things that God has done for you with them, then you've got a life.

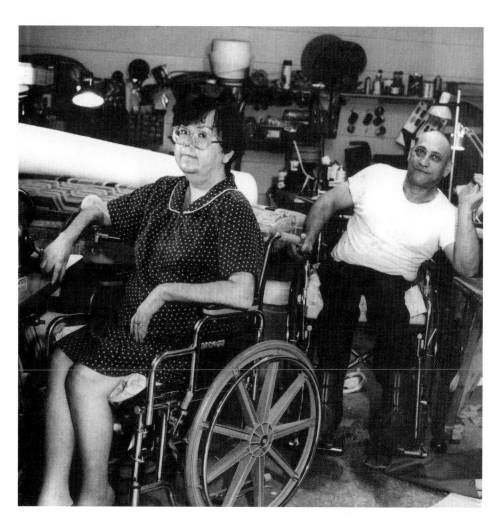

Janet Yates
Manager
Yates Upholstery Shop
Prater, Virginia

My father was killed by black lung. I lost four brothers to black lung. My first husband had black lung when he died, and my second husband died from black lung. If you could ever see a miner give his life up from black lung, you'd understand.

Once Jessie got black lung, there was no turning back; it didn't get any better. It only got worse, and there wasn't any cure. I lived it for ten solid years. I sat and watched my husband, Jessie E. Crabtree, die of black lung. Each day he got weaker, and it affected every organ in his body—his lungs, and his kidneys, and his heart. That's what black lung did to Jessie. He got so weak he couldn't even spit the mucus out of his throat. I had to sit there with a Kleenex and pull it out for him. I sat in the hospital for five long years, in and out, and every night he stayed, I stayed with him. I didn't leave him. I stayed by his bed. All that time he was waiting on his benefits. They awarded them in '79, but he didn't get them until '83. I've got the papers to prove it.

A man should draw his benefits while he's living. He shouldn't have to wait until he's dead. That's what hurts the women so much. After their husbands are gone, they don't get any compensation for his black lung. And that's wrong. They're not old enough to draw Social Security, and many a woman has been forced into a bad marriage because she didn't have any benefits and she had to take care of her little children. Why can't they pay those women, so they don't have to marry a man they don't love? It's not like they'd be giving them anything.

Women and children live in the coalfields, too, and they breathe coal dust just like the men do, and they end up with asthma. I even know some women who've died from black lung, but they couldn't get any compensation because they weren't coal miners. That's wrong. Everybody in the coalfields should have medical coverage—men, women, and children. They should all be treated equally.

Edith Crabtree
Black lung activist
Man, West Virginia

> *It was a once-in-a-hundred-year flood. We lost everything.*

We lost everything we had in the 1977 flood. We lost our homes, our cars, our pictures, our belongings. Everything. It rained for three days and three nights, and the ground was frozen. Trash and rubbish caught on the bridge at Loyall and turned the water a different way. Daddy's trailer floated across the gully and broke right down the middle. Half of it went up the gully, and the other half went down the creek. One of his houses and two of his rental trailers washed away. We had no flood insurance, because it had never flooded where we lived.

We'd just started a plumbing business, and we'd been in business about a year. The Small Business Administration refused to lend us anything, so all the money that was in the business was ours. We'd all been looking at the plumbing business as a family venture, but our dream got washed away. We'd gone into debt to buy some trucks, and when it was all over, all our power tools and all our trucks were gone. We lost an International van, a Chevrolet truck, a station wagon, and a Ford Ranger. We took the station wagon up the highway, but the flood washed the asphalt out from under the road and put it right back down into the floodwaters. The insurance didn't pay anything, and we only got $1,800 from the state. We lost $180,000, and it took us years to pay all our debts.

After we finally managed to get out of debt, we decided we needed something to call our own, so we bought a mobile home and moved it to the Holiday Mobile Home Park. Jim worked in the water treatment plant at the park, and on June 29, 1982, there was an explosion, and he was burned over three-fourths of his upper torso. At first we thought it was methane, but now we know it was vinyl chloride. He was in the hospital twenty-five days, and ever since then he's been disabled. His workmen's compensation paid the hospital bill, but we had a rough time getting the insurance company to pay his disability. We've really had to fight all of this, but our family is still intact, and we've still got a roof over our heads. The only thing that's seen us through is our faith in God.

We're Pentecostals and we go to the Church of God. We still feel like the Lord has work for us to do, and we're being drawn toward mission work. We may stay here or we may go to Virginia. We don't know yet where we'll go. Wherever we go, we want to do something we can feel satisfied about. We've been praying, and we know we'll come out on top, because we're survivors and we believe in the Lord.

Jeanette Gilpin
Bookkeeper
Holiday Apartments
Harlan, Kentucky

I moved to Kentucky in 1933, when I was fifteen. I was pregnant at the time, and my father got Arnold, my husband, a job at the mine, working on the tipple. He made eight dollars a week, and we had to live on a dollar a day. It was hard to get by on that dollar because we had to take out doctor bills and other expenses. Really, truly, I had it so hard in Tennessee. We got by a lot better up here on what we did get. I was having it awful. Times were hard. Lord, I reckon.

We had electricity, but we didn't have any coal. People were mining coal, but they couldn't afford to buy it from the company. They had to carry it from the river. And we had to buy everything at the company commissary, because we didn't have any money, just scrip. Sometimes we starved ourselves nearly to death so we could draw eight or nine dollars, but if they caught you spending it in town they fired you and made you move. They made us move once. It was after Arnold's leg was amputated. He was coming down the incline at the tipple, and he fell and lost his leg. They offered us eight hundred dollars and we took it. After that he wasn't able to work, and it was up to me to take care of the kids. I was a mother and father to all three boys, and it was rough.

After I divorced Arnold, I went to work as a janitor. There was a schoolhouse on Kitts Hill, and I kept it clean. It was a two or three mile walk, and I made a dollar a day. I went up there in the mornings and evenings and built fires. It was a one-room schoolhouse, but they had it partitioned off into three rooms with three stoves. They only taught to fifth grade. The reason schools only went to fourth and fifth grade was because by the time the boys got up that high, they were old enough to go into the mines, even if it was just picking up slate.

I started bootlegging in the 1950s so I could take better care of the boys. I didn't make moonshine. I sold bonded whiskey and beer. I bootlegged for eighteen years, until the boys were raised, and then I quit. It kept me off welfare, and I raised my three boys. Roy is a civil mining engineer for Great Western, Jimmy worked in the mines until he was disabled, and Jean's been sick all his life. I'm happier now than I ever was in my life. I don't have a man and don't want one. Every one I ever had treated me like a dog. All I ever wanted was enough to get by on and to be treated like a human being. Lord, it's been hard. I've not had an easy day in my whole life, but right now I feel pretty good.

Alta Whitaker
Survivor
Kitts, Kentucky

> *A miner's wife is always worried, but I did the best I could by my husband, I did the best I could by my children, I did the best I could by my neighbors, and I wouldn't change a thing.*

My father died when I was six days old. My mother worked for people to raise us children. She didn't marry again. I married Richard Nunn in 1928, when I was seventeen, and we moved to Harlan County and set up housekeeping at Coxston. I guess that was a happy time. We had plenty of everything. My husband was working for Koppers Coal Company and we moved into a coal camp. We raised our two children there, a boy and a girl. My husband worked in the coal mines for thirty-four years. He liked mining, but the rest of the family dreaded it because we never knew whether he was going to come home at night or not, and I was always worried. I never did get used to it. He worked in the mines until he retired. He did his last work at Blue Diamond Coal Company at Chevrolet.

He had work all the way through the Depression. Those were bad times. Nobody had anything. When Franklin D. Roosevelt got elected president, I handled more money than I'd ever seen in my life. President Roosevelt had everything to do with this county getting organized. Until he was elected, they couldn't get nowhere with the union. They had to slip around and try to get organized. But after he was elected, it was an open thing. John L. Lewis was the president of the United Mine Workers of America, and they organized the whole county. He saw to it that we had a closed shop, and that's when times got good. Everything was better for the laboring class of people. There was good times for several years; everybody had plenty and everybody's children went to high school. It was a good life in terms of people, but a hard life in terms of money. Whatever we got, we had to strike to get it.

The longest strike we ever had lasted nine months. My husband never missed a picket line. I took care of the house and I took care of the children. I got them up at four o'clock in the morning and took them to the picket line. The women didn't participate back then like they do now. If I was young enough, I'd go march in a picket line today. In 1969, my husband died from black lung, but I am well taken care of from his UMWA pension, black lung benefits, and Social Security. I also have an insurance card. Every time I go to the doctor, I only pay five dollars, and it pays for everything else. They don't keep us in the hospital as long as they used to, but they still take care of us. I'm a coal miner's wife, and I'm a dues paying UMWA member. I never worked in the mines, but they asked all of us pensioners to let them take so much out a month to help keep our hospital cards, and of course we all agreed. They sent me a card, and now I'm a dues paying union member.

**Hazel Nunn
Coal miner's wife
UMWA member
Lee County, Virginia**

> *When I need something, I don't call Clinton, I didn't call*
> *Reagan, and I didn't call Bush. I call my Heavenly Father.*
> *He takes care of me.*

Christ is first in my life. I'm an evangelist and I play music. I work with different churches; it doesn't make any difference to me. Every Sunday I play the piano at the Presbyterian church, and I've preached for the Holiness, but I'm the only licensed woman evangelist in the state of West Virginia. I was licensed by the National Baptist Convention. There's one Lord, one faith, and one baptism. Hallelujah!

I brought my first message to the Wingfield Baptist Church on Palm Sunday. Some people were upset, but I didn't let that stop me because I was baptized in a Baptist church, and God called me to lead, and I'm still there today, being blessed. I preach every Sunday, and people show up when I preach. While I was sitting at Hardee's eating, the Lord gave me a message on how to prepare for the coming of the Lord. Would you believe in less than twenty-four hours I had an invitation to preach? After I finished, the minister said we'd had a good church service, so the presence of the Lord was in that place.

The Lord's been good to us. My husband, Robert, was a coal miner and a small operator in the coal camp at Eckman. I've been in the same house for fifty-two years. It was a company house, and we rented four rooms for twelve dollars a month. Then we bought it through the bank for twelve hundred or eighteen hundred dollars, and we made it into eight rooms and put in a basement. We raised twelve children in that house—eight sons and four daughters. They all graduated from high school, and four of them graduated from college. I can't say it was hard to feed those twelve children; I knew how to manage, and we used what we had.

Robert was a good businessman. When he wasn't in the mine, he sold produce and he peddled chickens and he raised hogs. Robert even cleaned cesspools. Anything to turn an honest dollar. When the kids got of age, they worked, and I taught them how to act. I had to use the switch on them to let them know they had to mind me, so if that's child abuse, I'm guilty. The Bible says, "Spare the rod and spoil the child." They came in and they did their homework.

I would like to see things get better in McDowell County. I can't see it happening right now, but all things are possible with God. The Lord will work this out for us. I'm willing to put my faith in God. A lot of people talk about Democrats and Republicans, but I trust God.

Nannie B. Spencer
Minister
Eckman, West Virginia

PART TWO

APPALACHIAN MEMORIES

I remember going to my grandmother and grandfather's home for summer vacations when the trains still carried passengers and the ticket was under ten dollars. Our mother would sometimes get a ride for my sister and me with friends or acquaintances who were driving south. What must she have paid them if the train fare was about ten dollars that made it worth the trouble to take us with them? Knoxville, our destination, was on the way to Atlanta and ultimately Miami and work, so perhaps Mother gave ten dollars for the both of us, with a bit of lunch thrown in.

We owned a 1953 wintergreen Chevrolet, but our father worked at least two jobs and didn't have time to take us himself, and Mother did drive but never on the highways. Driving to Knoxville, "Gritsy" as Gary and I called it, was an all-day job. The old highway, 42E, was a two laner with signs saying PREPARE TO MEET THY GOD as you came around the mountainsides. Of course, when I was older I understood that the signs were because people were speeding and the turns were sharp, and at night drivers would hit the middle of the road driving with no lights but counting on the lights of the oncoming cars to tell them when to move over. Some made it but many didn't. Some were bootleggers; some were just unlucky.

But we didn't travel at night and we certainly didn't speed. Before the interstates there were also speed traps, and a group of black people traveling South did not have the money to bribe nor was it generally safe to have to encounter the sheriffs and judges in those small towns. I remember once when I myself was the driver on the way to New York. We got stopped in some small Pennsylvania town and were hauled before a judge. As we waited in the sheriff's office, which we recognized to be a huge courtesy, the judge finished washing her dishes and came downstairs drying her hands. Luckily we could pay the fine and were soon on our way. At another time this could have been a fatal encounter.

It was beautiful as we rode highway 42 between Cincinnati and Knoxville. We would always stop in Berea where we knew we would be able to fill up, use the bathroom, and get something to drink. We always remembered to take a carton of empty coke bottles when we left home so that when we made our halfway break at Berea we could take cold cokes with us while leaving the empties behind. In those days a nickel, which they would have charged us though the bottle was only worth two cents, made a difference and people did not waste.

When we pulled out of Berea, I would always notice the yards filled with chenille spreads and some of the most beautiful quilts I have ever seen. The quilts would be hanging in the front yards all the way down to Corbin, Kentucky. We didn't often stop, because even though the quilts were only selling for twenty-five dollars, none of us in the car had the money to spare. It was a joy about twenty years later to learn that the quilters had formed an Appalachian cooperative to sell their quilts for what they are worth. I recall the pride I felt, though I knew none of the women, when I saw the quilts on sale in Bloomingdales. Good for the women, I thought.

It was not easy being a woman in those days, and I don't think it is easy now. But they are strong and faithful and true. They deserve our respect for all the dreams they have dreamed that will never come to fruition. Those patches that they sewed into quilts to warm their families and ours are a testament to their faith in the future. Good for the women and the voices that form a chorus demanding justice and fair play for us and the land we live on.

Nikki Giovanni
Blacksburg, Virginia

> *When the coal company leaves, it leaves nothing behind;*
> *it leaves no support industry; it leaves no alternatives*
> *for employment and in a lot of places,*
> *it leaves wholesale destruction.*

The people in this area are very focused on the coal industry; there's a whole so-cial culture that's grown up around the mines. It's not an easy job; it's hard, dirty, dangerous work, but it pays twelve to seventeen dollars an hour, and if you're willing to take the trade-off, it gives you a higher standard of living. For most miners, how-ever, it isn't just a way to bring home a paycheck—they really like what they do. But unless something dramatic happens, like a tremendous increase in oil prices, I don't think the coal industry as we know it is going to last much longer; we're losing fifty jobs a month.

Part of that is due to the price that can be obtained for coal, five or ten dol-lars a ton less, and a large part is due to mechanization; one coal miner can do the job that it once took three to do. Only about a quarter of the miners are left that were here forty years ago. Mechanization is never going to go away, and coal is a fi-nite industry—when it's done, it's done, and it won't be possible to go back to the way it was before they started mining coal.

Back then, this area was a rural, very sparsely populated, subsistence farm-ing region. The coal industry changed it into a business center of sorts, but it's a very limited business center because it doesn't teach skills that go beyond the coal indus-try itself, and those skills don't transfer into other areas. It creates a temporary finan-cial security, bringing more income into the home, but people are very much aware that the coal industry is collapsing all around them, and that creates a lot of fear.

There are a lot of reasons for the decline in the coal industry. The easy seams have already been mined. There are tremendous coal reserves still here, but they're more expensive to mine unless they strip-mine, which is very quick and cost effec-tive but also very destructive. With the increased costs of labor, the increased costs of mining, and the decreased price that is paid for the finished product, this is not the profitable business that it once was.

Frankly, I despair for the future. As the coal industry continues to collapse, I hope other employment alternatives can be found. There's money available for re-training, but it's pointless to retrain people for jobs that don't exist. You can't just snap your fingers overnight and magically make a bunch of new industries appear. I think there's also a real question right now as to whether this region can be self-suffi-cient or whether it has to look outside of the area for support.

Susan Oglebay
Former attorney
United Mine Workers of America,
    District 28
Castlewood, Virginia

I'm the youth director, Elkhorn Valley Youth and Community Center, in Keystone. Three years ago we met in a church and tried to figure out what we could do for our youth, and we decided we needed a youth center to take them off the street, give them things to do, and help them develop a positive attitude. Since then, we've developed a number of programs. One of them is the Juvenile Justice Prevention Program.

They hired me as the youth director, and we've been working out of a double-wide trailer a church in Amondale gave us. The county gave us one of their old schools, Keystone Elementary; it's the biggest meeting place between Bluefield and Welch. Now we can accommodate young and old folks. It has a recreation room, gymnasium, and crafts center, and we use the cafeteria for home nursing programs and GED classes. We also do a two-day after-school tutoring program for grades K through 6, with an hour of tutoring, another hour of recreation, and a snack before we send them home.

The classrooms were overcrowded in the local school, and the kids weren't getting the one-on-one help they needed. After we helped them, their grades came up to B's and C's. We had the school give us a list of kids who needed tutoring, and there were ninety names on the list. We've managed to get twenty-five kids to the center so far, but a lot of them have transportation problems or their parents don't support what we're trying to do. I've tried to overcome that problem.

I went through the Woodson Leadership Program at Berea College, and they taught me how to involve the parents. They help with the tutoring, give drug-free dances, help secure the dances, and do the cleanup. The kids understand that if any problems occur during the dance the whole thing is shut down and they don't get their two dollars back. The last time we had a dance there were 180 kids, and they were real good. Once they left the school at midnight, they had to get off the street because they had a nine o'clock curfew.

I've worked with the Brushy Fork Institute for the past five years, helping put on workshops for people in McDowell County. We do teen leadership programs, work programs, self-esteem programs, AIDS awareness, and drug awareness. Drugs are more of a problem here than AIDS. We talk to them and do a drug-free safe camp. We asked them to draw pictures about what was safe and what was unsafe about their houses. They didn't draw too many unsafe things. Alcohol is a bigger problem than any other drug, and I see more neglect than abuse.

I want the kids to get an education and stay here and get jobs, so McDowell County can be a thriving community like it was years ago, with good jobs and decent houses.

Vondelere Scott
Youth director
Elkhorn Valley Youth
and Community Center
Keystone, West Virginia

> *God made the earth to take care of itself.*
> *Man has ruined it.*

I get up at five every morning, cook on a woodstove, work while it's daylight, and when it gets dark I go to bed. The Bible says, "If you have enough, be satisfied, and you'll have enough to live." I've always had enough, and I've had a good life. It couldn't have been any better. But it's never been easy. There were ten of us children, and we helped Dad and Mother farm 763 acres. We all knew our jobs and we all worked. I worked in the garden all day long.

I raised potatoes, onions, peas, beans, parsnips, beets, and carrots. And I took care of the orchard. We used to have all kinds of apples—red and golden delicious—and we raised chickens and turkeys and cattle and hogs. Every year we butchered several hogs. We killed them, strung them up, and gutted them. We stuffed the intestines and made sausage. They called them "mountain lobsters." We cleaned them real good and made chitlins. We salted some of the meat and put it in the storehouse, but mostly we canned sausage and part of the lean meat. We raised ten acres of corn, shucked it, and had it ground at the co-op in Grundy. In the wintertime we fed it to the stock. We milked and kept five hundred hens and sold the eggs to the hospital in Grundy. Seven cases a week . . . thirty dozen in a case . . . fifty cents a dozen. Feed was $3.75 and $4 a hundred back then, but now it's $15 a hundred. Then they changed the laws. They wanted everything graded and inspected. They told us we couldn't sell eggs unless we sold them to a company, but we couldn't make any money that way because companies get their feed a lot cheaper, so we quit selling eggs. The same thing happened to tobacco.

We raised an acre of tobacco for a cash crop, and they kept whittling down our acre until they got us down to a half acre. And then they put it on poundage. We were only allowed to sell so much, and they kept a record and wanted to know if we had any left over. When they weighed it at the market, they put down if you brought any back; then the next summer they came back to see if you still had that tobacco and what you'd done with it. Oh, well, I guess that's life. When you go, you won't take any of it with you, only your spirit.

On Sundays we went to the Boyd Ridge Methodist Church. Sometimes other churches came in and used our church for revivals. We let every church preach. I believe when we get to heaven, we're going to live with all churches. I've had a happy life. I don't know whether I could have done any better or not. I've been satisfied. I never thought about marrying. Whenever you marry there's two lines, and if you live by yourself there's just one line and you can do what you want. The Bible says contentment is great gain. If you're content with what you're doing, then you've got it. Don't ask for no more.

Sarah J. Barton
Mountain woman
Vansant, Virginia

> *When I think of the mines, I think of black lung,*
> *injuries, and death; life in the coalfields is hard,*
> *but if you live here, coal mining's your life.*

In 1937, when I was two, my father was killed in the mines. They didn't have a union, so my mother didn't get any benefits. She was pregnant with my youngest sister at the time, and she was forced to remarry. We moved from Kentucky to West Virginia, where my stepfather worked in the mines. Years later he died from black lung. The mines really affected me because mother had to go to work to help raise three girls. She really had a hard time; one payday she'd buy one pair of shoes, and the next payday she'd buy another pair. We lived payday to payday. I found out years later that some people had it worse.

My whole life has been affected by coal mining. My father was killed in the mines, and if my husband's father hadn't come here from Hungary to work in the mines, I wouldn't have met him. My stepfather died from black lung and my husband is disabled from a back injury and black lung. Even though my husband doesn't work anymore, we are still involved with coal mining, and we help out wherever we can. One of the most important things we do is working with a black lung organization.

The black lung laws were set up to compensate a man for losing his lungs, but it doesn't work that way. When a miner files for his black lung benefits, it's the beginning of a nightmare. The companies send him to doctor after doctor, trying to get a negative result. As it is now, they're only allowing maybe four out of a hundred claims. The other thing that hurt us was when they took away the presumption clause, which said that if a man worked ten years in the mines and had one piece of positive evidence, he was entitled to black lung benefits. They took that out several years ago, and the union has been trying to get it put back in ever since. My husband and I are strictly union.

During the Pittston strike we cooked for the miners. We started out making eighty ham salad sandwiches a day, but it really snowballed and we ended up serving two or three hundred people in two locations; we had beef stew, chicken and dumplings, and meat loaf. I'd make twenty-five meat loaves, ten pans of cornbread, and we'd haul it up there in our camper. The hardest part was doing the pots and pans. That lasted for thirteen months, and the only reason we quit was because my mother was put in a nursing home. We do whatever we can to help the union.

Any man who works in a coal mine is going to have black lung. There's no way around it because he's going to breathe dust, but the dust he sees is not what causes black lung—that dust gets caught in the hairs in his nose. What he breathes in is the dust he doesn't see, and it builds up in his lungs and forms nodules, which fill up his lungs. When it gets to the outer surface it turns them black, and he finally dies. It's horrible, but I have never heard any of the old coal miners say, "I wish I had never gone in the mines."

Cecile Szucs
Black lung activist
Stollings, West Virginia

I just look at myself as Gwen, not as an Appalachian woman, not as a black woman. I'm just Gwen.

Women around here are very, very strong. There's a lot of black women professionals with good jobs. That's the message I try to get across to young mothers. Even if they've had a child out of wedlock, I tell them it isn't the end of the world. I was a single parent. I had to be a strong woman to survive, and they can be strong women, too. It is definitely the women, black women and white women, that make this town. If we had to depend on the men around here, we wouldn't have anything, and I think a lot of that has to do with their education.

Somewhere between kindergarten and twelfth grade, a lot of the men, black and white, missed the purpose of life. They've been out of work ten years, and they haven't done anything with their lives. Instead of going to a community college for a two-year degree, they stand around on the street corners and brag about how much liquor they can drink. It's part of a vicious cycle, and it's so sad—the alcohol, the drugs, and the violence. I'm not willing to say Appalachian men are more violent than other men, but I do think they've lost their sense of pride.

Along with missing their goal in life, I think they were also raised with the idea that things should stay the way they were in the old coal mining days, when Daddy went off to work and Momma stayed home and raised a houseful of kids. They haven't figured out it's not that way today. Women are more educated, and men fear them because they think they're a threat to their masculinity. The men haven't gone anywhere, and they think it's supposed to be that way. When they meet an educated woman, they're afraid of her.

Appalachian women have always struggled against that fear, and that's what makes them unique. They have to be twice as good, because they're struggling against two things: their own men's ideas from the past and the myths people have about women from the region. When I meet someone from New York or Boston and I tell them I'm from Harlan County, or more specifically, Lynch, Kentucky, they automatically think I'm a hillbilly with a corncob pipe and a straw hat. That's a hard stereotype to overcome, and it makes it harder for me to teach.

When I was in school we were taught respect and morals, and we were taught about God. These days I'd get into trouble if I said a prayer. I don't understand this generation. They're not raising their children; they're just having babies and feeding them, and some of them aren't even getting fed. I don't have a solution, but I know what I'd like to do. If I could find a magic bottle and rub it, and a genie came out and he promised me anything I wanted, I'd ask for motivation for boys and girls. Get up and break the cycle. Don't waste your brains or your lives. Get motivated. You can be whatever you want to be.

Gwendolyn D. Jackson
Teacher
Lynch, Kentucky

> *We've cried a lot, and we've laughed a lot,*
> *but we've stuck together, and we've survived.*

My husband, Glen, was twenty-six when he started working in the mines. His father and my family had all been miners, and we'd moved back home from South Carolina so he could go to work in the mines. He'd only worked there for five years when he was injured in a roof fall in November 1978. He didn't have a canopy over his bolting machine, and the rocks crushed his spinal cord. He became a paraplegic—at thirty-one.

We had a terrible time adjusting to the accident, particularly since the holidays were close. We'd planned for Glen to come home for Christmas. We had the house all decorated; the tree was up, the lights were up, and we were going to prepare a big meal, like we did every Christmas. Then he got blood clots in his legs, and he couldn't come home. After we found out, we loaded up the tree, the lights, and all the gifts and carried them to our room on the fifth floor of Howard Johnson's in Charlottesville. We warmed up peas and mashed potatoes in coffee pots, and when Glen came over from the hospital, we had turkey with all the trimmings.

When Glen came home, the UMWA took up a collection from the union miners, and they built a ramp for Glen's wheelchair, but the house wasn't fixed for a paraplegic. We went back to the insurance company to see if they would help remodel the house, but they said they wouldn't because the law didn't require them to. I got mad. I told them Glen hadn't asked for this, and I felt like the coal industry, if it was willing to put a man or woman in danger, should be willing to take care of them when they got hurt. I told them the law was wrong and needed to be changed.

I discovered it was easier to make a law than change a law, but I didn't give up. I got busy, and I started pushing. By the time I got the compensation law changed, I found out it wouldn't help Glen, but that was all right because it helped other people. Glen and I didn't give up. We kept working on things close to home. The high school in Wise didn't have ramps, and he couldn't see football games or watch his daughter play basketball. We got that changed. Now we're working on getting the aisles cleared in stores at the local shopping centers, but it won't be easy. None of this has been easy. It's been tough in a lot of ways.

It's been tough on Glen, because people wanted to pity him, but he wouldn't let them. He's very independent. It was tough on me, because I thought I was Superwoman, and when I found out I couldn't fix everything, I got real bitter, and that made it tough on our girls, particularly the oldest one. Financially, it was hard, and that made it tough on us as a family, but we've survived. My main goal now is to see that the handicapped get equal treatment. I don't care if they're in a wheelchair or deaf or blind. They're the same person they were before, and they've got the same heart, and they should be treated the same.

Nila P. Bolling
Handicapped rights activist
Wise, Virginia

> *During the Ravenwood strike, if these companies had known
> what they were doing for the labor movement, they'd have
> given us a contract, just like if Pilate had known what he was
> doing for Christianity, he would never have had Jesus killed;
> he'd have chosen Barabus instead.*

When I was growing up, our house was always filled with music. Sometimes we would play and sing all night long. Mom's family gathered at our house in shifts throughout the night, beginning at five or six o'clock in the evening, and they went right on through until five or six the next morning. I was only two or three at the time, and while this was going on I slept in a baby bed behind the big Warm Morning stove. We also had a double open fireplace with a metal grate built in cement, and we baked potatoes next to the hot coals all night long.

When I was five years old, I stood on a big rock in my Grandpa Shelton's front yard and sang for a crowd of twenty or more. I loved it. I was in all the talent shows and plays in school. As teenagers, my brother Ira and I would sing country music as a duet and mix it with fifties and sixties rock and roll. People came from all around to hear us play. Ira is a real good singer and, even though he was only sixteen, he was one of the best guitar players in the state. Ira's like Daddy—he can play anything. As we got older, Ira and I grew apart. He went to Vietnam, and I went to Washington, D.C., to work. I sang some in D.C., and he sang some in the service, but he had lost all interest in music by the time he came home from Vietnam. Since I'd never played on my own, I thought that was the end of my music career.

Years later, after eighteen years of marriage and three children, my husband, Bethel, bought a guitar for me at Christmas, and I started playing with Daddy. Before, I had always sung, but I'd never played because there were too many musicians around for me to go out of my way to make a fool of myself. I'd just tell them to play on; I'm a singer, not a picker. But when everyone was gone, I practiced with Daddy. My fingers were too small for the neck of the guitar, so Daddy worked out a way for me to put enough pressure on the strings to make a clear sound. I thought my thumb would drop off, but I could sound the chords clearly. He taught me how to listen for chord changes, high or low, and go into the change with what my voice was doing. I got to where I could hear harmonies in the sounds of different strings. I still use that tool today when I'm having a difficult time finding a particular harmony sequence.

After I started playing on my own, I started writing my own material, playing at strikes, giving concerts, and recording music. I've also worked with the West Virginia Justice Project and the American Friends Service Committee, which tries through education and conflict resolution methods to gain basic rights for all people through empowerment. I also work with Black Lung Organization in West Virginia, West Virginians for Health Care Rights, and the West Virginia Homelessness Project through the Catholic Community Services Organization and the United Methodist Churches of West Virginia. I thank God for giving me my talent, but if I don't use it to help people make their lives better, He could just as easily take it away.

46

Elaine Purkey
Singer and songwriter
Chapmanville, West Virginia

> *I'm not sure I'll ever be from here, but when I pass away,*
> *they're going to know I was here.*

While my husband was president of the United Mine Workers, we traveled in the coalfields of Kentucky, Virginia, West Virginia, Pennsylvania, Illinois, and Indiana. We also traveled out west and in Canada, and while we were there we often stayed in people's homes, and I learned a lot from the women I met. Most of them were normally soft-spoken and very family-oriented, but when it came to changing a safety regulation, strengthening a law, or getting textbooks for their children, the women hung together. They were always out front organizing and making changes. When they put their shy voices together, they became very loud, booming voices, and they gave me strength.

When Sam lost the international election, we left Fairfax County and came back to the coalfields of southwestern Virginia. I didn't understand why it was so important for Sam to raise our son here, but now I do—Nathaniel's happy and healthy and productive. He's all the things a parent could ask for; he's an honors student, a good leader, a wonderful child, and he gets along well with people. Every year, when the legislature's in session, I take him to Richmond for a week so he can see how his government works. I'm not sure he'll stay here, but I think he'll put something back into the community. That kind of commitment is very strong in our family.

Some of my neighbors think I'm a little bit too radical or a little bit too outspoken. At the same time, I think they have a pretty healthy respect for me. I have some pretty deep roots in working folks; my mother is from south Georgia, and when she was two, my grandfather died, and my grandmother raised four children, basically as a sharecropper. My grandmother wasn't interested in a lot of money or a lot of power. She wanted to lead a useful, productive life, and so do I. I've tried to follow her example.

Patti D. Church
Community activist
Appalachia, Virginia

> *People have learned they can't depend on the big companies*
> *to do things for them. They're going to have to start*
> *doing things for themselves.*

Wilcoe is a black and white community, but the section where I grew up was called Newtown, and it was basically black. There were only fourteen houses on both sides of the highway. Growing up there was fun. Until third grade, I walked to the little school in Wilcoe, and I went to class with black and white students. Later, I caught the school bus and went to Main Gary until sixth grade. After integration, I went to Gary High School. I liked the bigger school because there were more things going on. Even though Gary was just two miles up the road, we never got to go, and when we caught the bus, it was like moving up.

My father died from a cerebral hemorrhage when I was in fifth grade. Now they would say he was an alcoholic, but then they just said he had a drinking problem, or they didn't say anything at all. To me, he was a wonderful dad. He didn't hit us. Sometimes he came home drunk and he fussed, but nothing major. He was an only child, and that was the reason he wanted a big family. He loved the holidays.

My mother didn't remarry, and it took her two years to get her black lung, Social Security, and veterans' benefits from Dad's service in the Korean War. I have good memories. My mom was a homemaker; she also did day work and worked at a restaurant when I was growing up. One time, when I was small, she went to New York and worked, but she didn't stay long before she returned. All eleven of us graduated from high school, and four of us graduated from college. I had five brothers; my father and all of them served in the army. It was a part of our life that they went into the service and then came back. Only one of them had any trouble.

I'm a prenatal counselor at the health clinic. We provide women in the community with education and prenatal and postpartum care services. We bring them into the clinic and try to help them deliver healthy babies. We get referrals from girls who come in and get positive pregnancy tests. The rates showed a slight decrease for awhile—now they're up again. But we have many success stories. These girls pass their GED tests and go to a vocational school where they take business courses or train to be an LPN. Their futures are bright because they're able to find jobs.

I also work with older women who have problems with electrical bills or paying the rent or substandard housing. Sometimes I'm just their friend. I can pick ten women and the only thing they have in common is no money. They have lots of problems, but each one is little different. When the mining companies pulled out there weren't any jobs, and a lot of people had to go on welfare. These were people whose parents and grandparents had never been welfare recipients—they were workers. Unfortunately, the mines didn't give back to McDowell County what McDowell County gave to them; they robbed and they took, and the only thing U.S. Steel left behind was the football field!

Dameta J. Brown
Prenatal counselor
Tugg River Health Clinic
Gary, West Virginia

> *Next week we're turning on the water.*

In the early 1960s, I heard the VISTA message that Appalachia was a second-rate place, full of second-rate people. For some reason, I bought into that message and moved to Washington, D.C. I worked for a law firm, made good money, visited museums, saw lots of plays, and attended the opera. I loved it. I stayed four years, until I reached a point where I couldn't deal with the homeless.

I ignored them like everyone else; I acted like I didn't see them or hear them or didn't understand their misery. Then one day I passed a little black girl who was pregnant, and she was begging. I had passed up hundreds of people, but for some reason, I couldn't pass her up. I took her to my law firm, and we got her set up in a mission. I found out later she had a baby boy and they were both fine, but I wasn't. After I finally opened that door, it just ate me up inside, and I came home and went to work for the UMWA as a field service representative. I helped people get their health care cards and benefits.

I also helped organize the McDowell County Health Education Program. We wanted to teach people to take better care of themselves so they wouldn't need a doctor as often. One of our major problems was clean water. The Olga Coal Company owned the water company until the mid-fifties. When they sold it to the several partners who formed the McDowell County Water Company. When the water company went bankrupt in 1988, they sold out to Thomas Blair III, a rich, politically powerful Charleston businessman. Within three months, I had worms coming through my faucets, the water contained coal, wood, and feces, and it was bacterially contaminated.

Things finally got so bad in Coalwood and Caretta that people banded together to get things done. They chose to prosecute a criminal case, pursue a civil case, and get the county commission to form a public service district. It took a lot of time, but we finally forced the courts and the agencies involved to put the water company, a private utility, in receivership. They actually took it away from the owner, Thomas Blair III. He'd bragged that he hadn't been to McDowell County for nine years and didn't plan on coming back. He was pretty unhappy when they drug him down here the first time and took away his $250,000 investment, but he was even more unhappy when they drug him down here a second time and threw his butt in jail.

In November 1990 the McDowell County Public Service District was formed. I was appointed chairperson, and we developed a long-range strategic plan that would solve our water problem. The first phase was to replace, from the ground up, all water systems in the fifteen communities that had been served by the McDowell County Water Company. The second phase was to do the same thing for the rest of McDowell County. Our funding was provided by the FHA, the Economic Development Administration, the governor's office and the Soil Conservation District.

52

Frances Patton Rutherford
Chairperson
McDowell County Public Service District
Caretta, West Virginia

> *They don't care about you after you're old and gone. . . .*
> *They're after the new feller to do him in.*

When my mother and I put in our applications at Birchfield in 1972, they thought we wanted office work. When they found out we wanted to work in the mines, they tried to discourage us. The boss said the shaft where we'd be working was lower than his desk. We told him we didn't mind because we'd worked in sewing factories for minimum wage, and as far as we were concerned, that was lower, because it's slavery.

Three years later they hired me, and they sent me to the lowest coal. When my first paycheck came they only paid me for the one day I'd spent underground, not the training. They didn't pay me until the next payday, because they didn't think I'd stay. They thought I'd quit in the low coal. At first the guys were sort of cold, but after I worked with them awhile and they saw that I didn't dodge the mudholes, we got along real good. I learned from Daddy what hard work was.

Daddy's leg was off below the knee; he wore an artificial leg, not a good one like they have today. He hand-loaded coal on his hands and knees, and they didn't get paid for any rock they loaded. He worked long hours for two dollars a day or less. He worked in a union mine, but when he got sick he didn't draw a pension or get any hospitalization. That's when my mother, even though she was in her forties, went to work in the mines so we could maintain the same standard of living. She took over Dad's job, the same one he'd been doing. I was the first woman in the Birchfield mine. My mother was the second. We worked there for five years, until they shut it down.

When I started back to work in the mines at Moss 40, I ran a Wilcox Miner. The bridges weren't powered by machinery; the operator used a rope and a lever to work the bridges by hand up into the face. It was very hard labor, and I decided I wanted to run a shuttle car and compete with my husband. I bid the job, but one of the bosses refused to post me on the board. By the time I came out of my bathhouse the guys were all gathered around the office. We worked it out. They let me drive a "man trip," which is battery-operated and the next thing to a shuttle car. The guys backed me a hundred percent, and it made me feel good. Later on they let me run my shuttle car, and we started moving a lot more coal. I'd made my point. I didn't realize it at the time, but I should have filed a discrimination complaint. I learned I had to take action to protect my rights. That's what happened at Pittston.

We struck Pittston because they'd taken health care away from our pensioners. We worked fourteen months without a contract and finally struck on April 5, 1989. About two weeks later thirty-nine women took over Pittston's headquarters. We went in the front door at nine o'clock one morning and came out the same way at five o'clock the next day. They talked about using tear gas, but they were afraid of the crowd at the foot of the hill. In late February 1990, we won the strike and went back to work.

54

Catherine Tompa
Displaced miner
Cleveland, Virginia

> *We're not radicals. We're just mainstream people with a vision for positive change.*

I lived the first four and half years of my life on Paint Creek, in a two bedroom house. I thought the coal mines were terrible because of the mud and dirt, but I knew it fed us and kept us clothed. Up until adulthood I was ashamed of mining; I even detested it. But one time, as a young adult, Dad took me to a mine, and I thought finally I'll learn something about mines. When I got to the mouth of the mine, it was so cold, black, and drafty, I couldn't go in. At that point, I learned a new respect for what my dad had done all those years.

When I started school, I went to Livingston Elementary. Learning wasn't much fun, but something positive came out of that place. Back then we didn't have special education classes, and I went to school with the retarded and people with vision problems and lots of other handicaps. About that time I realized that, like those children, I was different; I was a coal miner's daughter, and I lived up a hollow, and there were people who were more professional than my Dad. Later on, I realized we had other things that were more important. We learned values that carried over into our lives, in community work and community service. Dad was always trying to do whatever he could do to help other people, and I'm a lot like him. When something needed to be done he did it, and so do I.

I'm a facilitator. I see us creating a situation in McDowell County where everything will be done at a central location. It will be a place for both individuals or families where services won't have to be duplicated. It will allow us to pool all our resources; schools could service the handicapped there, and we could help older people who have had strokes and need physical therapy. This strategic plan will service all the needs of the people in McDowell County, but it's going to take a lot of work. First we need to diversify economically, then unify socially, because for so long we've been fragmented, isolated, existing in pockets. Diversification will get us away from the dependency we've had on the coal industry, and we've formed an organization to help us unify. We call it McCAN, McDowell County Action Network, and through that organization we are both advocating and demanding our due.

Politically, we're trying to overcome past practices where politicians made deals to get something for themselves, or for what they thought was for the county; they traded a three-lane highway for Berwin Lake. Our lack of progress had a lot to do with red tape, and it had a lot to do with conflicts of interest. Certain factions always controlled the county, and now those factions are breaking down. I'm part of the new group; I'm on the Economic Development Board. But I've always known that everything starts with economic development; that's where we get mini-grants for workshops, community development, and grass-roots organization. If we keep working together, I think we're going to make it.

Deborah King
Teacher and activist
War, West Virginia

> *I see drama as a vehicle for community change. I'm determined to provide the children with more workshops, better workshops, and more professionals who will come in and educate them.*

In 1986, Charlene O'Hara started the Jellico Children's Theater. When she moved to Texas, the Mountain Women's Exchange adopted the theater and I became the director. At first, fundraising was difficult; we raised money with dances, bake sales and yard sales. Now, we receive small amounts of money from various arts organizations. My budget is a little over thirty-six thousand dollars a year. Sometimes we are able to raise the money, and sometimes we aren't. When we don't, we start pinching pennies and cutting back.

Our first play, *White Line,* was about drug abuse. The cast consisted of forty-eight high school students who came from Jellico, White Oak, Little Elk, and Elk Valley. It's difficult to get around in the mountains, so six or seven of them carpooled at a time just to get here, and that made me very proud, because it showed they were committed and excited about doing the play. They wrote the play themselves, and they performed it at the high school in front of a standing-room-only crowd. There are no art, music, or drama programs at the local high school, so this gave them an opportunity to get the credits they needed to graduate. I've worked with four students who are majoring in drama in nearby colleges.

The first workshop we participated in was put on by the Oak Ridge Community Theater at the Hilton Hotel in Knoxville. The children were amazed by the hotel, but they were also scared because it was the first time they'd performed in front of strangers. The workshop director was from New York, and he told them to sit on the floor and think about their worst fears. Later, he made them stand up and reveal their fears to the audience. One girl had recently been to a doctor who thought she might have cancer, but she was afraid to go back and see him because of what he might tell her. She cried. Another girl was afraid she would never marry and would spend the rest of her life alone. One of the young men was deathly afraid of snakes. He told the audience he could not stand the sight of snakes.

After the workshop was over, the director told them that what he'd been doing was teaching them to express themselves. He said that he knew that was difficult for teenagers. He also told them he knew that they didn't like to hug and kiss but that they should realize there was nothing wrong with that. After the workshop, one of the kids gave me a hug and a kiss, and he said, "Thank you for today!"

Jean E. Moses
Director
Jellico Children's Theater
Jellico, Tennessee

> *The people who stayed behind can make a real contribution because they haven't forgotten their relationship to the land.*

In 1967, because I had given my life to the people, not the church, I left the Glenmary Home Missioners and moved to Clairfield, Tennessee, where the population had dropped from twelve thousand to twelve hundred. Shortly after I arrived, several of us organized a nonprofit organization, Alliance for Communities Service, to help the people. Vanderbilt medical students provided summer health fairs, and their law students did a systematic search of who owned the land. They discovered that the people who owned 90 percent of the land paid only 4 percent of the taxes. That started my long, slow journey into understanding land issues as well as corporate, absentee land companies and their lack of ethics.

When we tried to find land for an industrial site, we wrote letters to the seven companies who owned land and asked them if they could find it in their hearts to sell us five or ten acres of land for an industrial park. Two of them wrote back and said it was against their policy to sell land, and the other five didn't even answer the letter. Later, when we tried to establish a clinic, we asked the American Association, an English company, if we could lease or buy one-half acre of their forty thousand for a clinic, and they said, "Absolutely not. We're not making any land available for you communists."

Eventually we managed to get a factory, a clinic, and to build three houses, but then we ran out of land. Over time, we grew to understand that we couldn't just get land for houses; we had to have enough land to generate some income. But we wanted to do it in a way that was environmentally sound. Ten years later, we formed a nonprofit, or community ownership, land trust, and any land we bought was held in trust for the community. We discovered we could lease the coal, oil, and timber the same way the land companies had leased them, but we decided we only wanted to work with the timber because coal, oil, and gas are extractive industries that won't renew themselves.

We're close to a brink. The rich are getting richer and the poor are getting poorer. As fossil fuels die out, food costs will go up and people will try and produce their own food, but they won't have the land to do it on because the rich will have bought up the land for vacation homes. Unfortunately, when people get angry enough, the rich will be perfect targets, and we'll see bloodshed, poverty, and chaos. By the time they figure out a new method of crop production, we're going to have as many starving Americans as we've seen starving Africans.

Marie Cirillo
Catholic Diocese of Knoxville
Appalachian Community Development
Woodland Community Development
  Corporation
Clairfield, Tennessee

PART THREE

WOMEN OF CAUSES

Historians tell us the Industrial Revolution transformed the workplace and redefined the domains and activities of men and women. Men were no longer employed at home. They went to work—in factories, offices, mills, and mines. The places where men toiled were *workplaces*. Women remained at home typically. And although they were mistresses of everything domestic (cooking, cleaning, child rearing), what they did was not considered work, for the home was not the workplace. The Industrial Revolution confined women to the home and cut them off from roles in business, industry, and government. Certainly the industrial incursion of the 1880s changed the lives of women in the region. That incursion may be said to have begun when William Barton Rogers, founder and first president of the Massachusetts Institute of Technology, died while speaking at the institute's commencement exercises. His last words were "bituminous coal." The year was 1882. For the most part the historians are correct. But this generalized view of our history leaves out all the women who combined their domestic roles as wives, mothers, and homemakers with roles in the workplace outside the home; women whose experiences at home, and in the workplace outside the home, involved them in causes and issues associated with business, industry, and government.

Such women tell their stories in *Women of Coal*. And because they share their stories, we have a more accurate view of our past, a better understanding of our present, and a more realistic hope for the future. Much that has been written about Appalachia depicts women as confined and suppressed by a male-dominated culture. I do not find that stereotype confirmed by the experiences, activities, or views of these women. Nor do these women see themselves in the stereotype. Geneva Steele, an activist from Paynesville, West Virginia, says: "Women are better at meetings. They're more apt to sit down and work at things and see both sides of an issue." Helen K. Carson, retired director of a Head Start program in Coalwood, West Virginia, thinks women are weathering change better than men: "Women are accepting new changes and adapting to them, while men are sticking to, and stuck in, traditional political forms. Women are rapidly taking over the old power positions and they're doing it with zeal and enthusiasm." Gwen Jackson, a teacher from Lynch, Kentucky, says, "Women around here are very, very strong." These women display admirable qualities. They are articulate and resourceful. "Then I got smart," Ruth Bush Anderson says as she relates how she learned to deal with a clerk at the company store. "At first we were very naive," Joan Robinett says, telling about the Dayhoit Citizens Group's efforts to clean up toxic waste. She got smart too, and her efforts, and those of the citizens group, resulted in a waste site being placed on the EPA's Superfund list.

These are women who learn from experience, who reflect, who have organizational and administrative skills, and who are full of leadership ability. They are hardly cut off from issues and collective concerns. Edith Crabtree, for example, is concerned with the issues of black lung benefits and medical coverage for workers. And these women are often aware that the issues that concern them are part of a larger picture. Linda Lester, a coal miner from Appalachia, Virginia, helped form the Coal Employment Project for Women. "The things that are happening here are happening all over the world," she says. Patricia M. Hatfield, director of the Buchannon County Public Library in Grundy, Virginia, sees Appalachia as part of the global community. She says, "I see accessibility to information as a way to tie Appalachia into what is going on in that community." At the same time, she thinks it is important to retain a sense of Appalachian culture, especially the attachment to the land and the attachment Appalachian people feel to one another, and to " balance who we are with what we want to be." These women are giving and caring, and they care about the things that matter: family, work, community. As Cosby Totten says, "Work gives people their dignity."

These women of coal don't simply submit to things as they are or have been, and they are not weighed down by the past; rather, they use knowledge of the past to address issues in the present and to build a better future. Lindia Gaile Fee uses a Jack tale to talk to young people about problem drinking. She considers herself a traditional mountain woman, but she uses her knowledge of the past "to help me in my daily life and to help build a future for myself and my family." There are no stereotypical women here, only complicated, persevering, enduring women. Wives, mothers, and homemakers, they are also coal miners, secretaries, teachers and counselors, attorneys, librarians, social workers, writers, singers and storytellers, ministers, youth and theater directors, owners and operators of businesses, and community leaders. They are survivors—of floods, fires, economic downturns and layoffs, unemployment, explosions that killed fathers, husbands—survivors sustained by religious faith, devotion to family, and sheer determination. And their determination is not only to survive but to grow and to achieve. Connie Childress, a teacher from Vansant, Virginia, says: "I want excellence to be the premier feature of my endeevars."

We have seen the likes of these women in nonfiction portraits of Appalachian women found in Horace Kephart's *Our Southern Highlanders,* John C. Campbell's *The Southern Highlander and His Homeland,* and Emma Bell Miles's *The Spirit of the Mountains.* They also remind me of fictional characters such as Harriette Arnow's Gertie Nevels from *The Dollmaker,* who when she appears afraid to enter a doctor's office is told by a soldier who has just watched her perform a roadside tracheotomy on her child, "Lady, you can't be afraid of nothing." I am reminded of Lydia McQueen, the protagonist in Wilma Dykeman's *The Tall Woman,* who struggles to maintain her home, family, and community during and after the Civil War, and of Alpha Baldridge in James Still's *River of Earth,* who, to rid herself of her husband's relatives, burns the house down and moves the family into the smokehouse. These women of coal, like Dykeman's heroine, are all tall women who cast long shadows into the futures of their communities. We all stand taller and are strengthened and empowered by knowing their stories.

Jim Wayne Miller
Bowling Green, Kentucky

Don't ever tell me I can't do something, because that's just going to make me work that much harder.

Even though I always wanted to be a doctor, my career didn't start off in medicine. I taught school for a year, and I worked for eight years in the accounting department at U.S. Steel. I was the first black ever to work in their main office. I was proud of what I'd done, but I was still interested in medicine. After eight years, I started working evenings in the Emergency Room at Logan General Hospital. At first, I couldn't read the doctors' writing, and I didn't understand the terminology, but I learned quickly and I loved it. Later on, I worked in Outpatient, Admissions, Pediatrics, and I eventually became an assistant administrator in Radiology. I did that for ten years, until Dr. Wolfe convinced me to enroll in a physicians' assistant program at Alderson Broadus College. That's how I became a physicians' assistant.

Now I work at Tugg River Clinic in Gary as the medical provider. I work with men, women, and children. If I have a problem patient, I discuss that patient with my supervising physician. I don't discuss every patient with him because I do my own diagnosis and treatment. I'm the only female health care provider in McDowell County. We have a lot of young people, especially women, who don't feel comfortable having males do their annual Pap smears and mammographies. I feel I'm helping reach a lot of women who would not otherwise go in for their annual examinations. But I also relate well with my male patients. I can somehow get men to do things other doctors can't get them to do. I once convinced a man who weighed 500 pounds that he needed to lose weight, and now he's down to 250!

A lot of my patients don't have any insurance, so they don't seek the health care they need. Our teen pregnancy rate is also very high, and sexually transmitted diseases are a real problem. These kids are setting themselves up for big trouble. The highest AIDS death rate is for males between nineteen and forty. We've tried to solve that problem by going into the schools one day a week and offering a school-based clinic. While we're there, we do behavior risk assessments, and for those children who are at high risk from their behaviors, we have permission from their parents to bring them back to the clinic, treat them, then take them back to school. Hopefully, this type of program will help cut down on the AIDS epidemic and stop a lot of other diseases. I love people. I've helped quite a few of them, and I'll continue doing so.

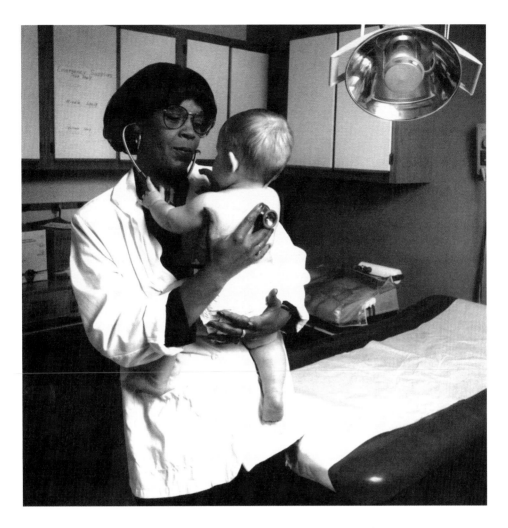

Pamela Ramsey
Physicians' assistant
Tugg River Health Clinic
Gary, West Virginia

My most memorable experience was when I was about five years old, sitting on the steps of my little house, wondering what was beyond those mountains. And that's been my life— looking beyond mountains to see what's out there.

My father was a Cherokee Indian, and I began studying Native American culture a couple of years ago. I found an old census that went back to 1800s, and I found my father's family there, on the Quala Indian Reservation. I was drawn to that reservation even though I didn't know what my father's roots were. While I was walking through the Indian village for tourists, there was a man burning a canoe from a big tree trunk, and my daddy could have passed for his twin brother.

The Black Wolf Clan was formed to help interracial and intercultural education in this area. Members in the group come from all walks of life . . . teachers, government workers, and blue-collar workers. It's been very interesting to me. My father never wanted to talk about his Indian heritage. The ones who went to Oklahoma on the Trail of Tears were considered brave ones, and the ones who stayed behind and hid out in the mountains were considered cowardly. They've always been persecuted. They've been robbed of their lands and their traditions and their language. They were punished for speaking their language in school, and now they're being robbed of their spiritual heritage—the new age movement is drawing in every Indian symbol and everything good the Indians stood for, and they're incorporating it into their own movement. And there's also the issue of commercialism. Cherokees have been turned into gazing stock, like a zoo. They resent all that commercialism, and yet it's the only way they have to make any money, which is ironic because a lot of it isn't even theirs; they don't own the shops.

I met a woman on the reservation a couple of years ago. She said her mother was buried at Jackson, Kentucky. She told me that when she went to look for her mother's grave, her heart was broken, because when she found the grave, there was a marker that said, simply, "Indian Woman." The burial mounds had been desecrated, and shopping malls and highways had been built. There's a girl from this area, a full-blooded Cherokee Indian, and she said they were taught to hide it all their lives. Those are the kinds of things we're fighting against.

Native Americans have been neglected Americans. We need to get rid of the stereotypes of the Indians as the bad guys, created in the Westerns, and bring the truth out about what the culture was really like. The Cherokee from the beginning were highly civilized. They never lived in tepees; they always built houses. The Spanish, under de Soto, taught the Indians how to scalp people, and the stories about the Indians being given blankets infected with smallpox are true. On the positive side, we owe our system of government to the Indians; the Iroquois Confederation was what our constitution was modeled after. Native American culture should be esteemed, not despised, and that's why I continue to learn about my heritage by reading, studying, visiting the reservation, and meeting with the Black Wolf Clan.

Wilma D. Boggs
Clan mother
Black Wolf Clan
Harlan, Kentucky

> *They say they're saving this coal, but I don't know*
> *what they're saving it for. They're destroying*
> *the people working it, and when they come back,*
> *I don't think they'll have a workforce.*

After I got my associate's degree in mining technology from Southwest Community College, my husband didn't want me to work in the mines, so I hung my degree over the sink and washed dishes. It was a strange situation; then he started coming around. He said he didn't care if I worked in the engineering department, but when I put in an application at Clinchfield, all they had were underground jobs. The next week they called me to work. He was still against it, but he'd just quit a job, and we had a big fight. He told me it wasn't any of my business where he worked! So I told him it wasn't any of his business where I worked.

At first I was scared to death. If he'd asked me to quit I would have, but he didn't ask, so I decided they'd have to carry me out of there dead because I wasn't giving up. I started at Clinchfield's training mine, and the first piece of equipment I drove was a scoop. It wasn't much different than driving a car; there was a gas and brake pedal, lights, and a directional switch for forward or reverse. While I was there, I did everything. After the training program, they sent me to Splashdam.

Most of the men at Splashdam had worked with women before, so it wasn't too bad. The older men didn't seem to have a problem with it at all. It was the younger men, more my own age, who had the problem; it was an ego, macho thing with them. But even the younger miners were willing to show me how to operate the equipment. I found out later from women at the conferences that there were a lot of problems at the other mines; they kept the women off the equipment, on the beltlines and out of the face. That wasn't a problem at Splashdam.

My first job was belt cleaner, but after a few months they put me on bridge carrier. It runs on tracks and follows the continuous miner wherever it goes; it forms a bridge between the miner and the beltline so that the coal flows continuously. Until I was laid off I ran a shuttle car. I ran around looking for people and looking for bad top over my head, listening for it to work. The people who run the shuttle cars are the movingest people on the section; they're always going somewhere. It's not hard work, but it's constant motion and its's never the same; I'm always negotiating new turns.

I worked for twelve years before I got laid off. I made almost seventeen dollars an hour, but I didn't save any money. Now I'm eligible for six months of unemployment, and if the government agrees we lost our jobs because of foreign competition, I'll be eligible for 108 more weeks. I'm most comfortable in the mines, but I've got to face reality; there just aren't any coal mining jobs out there. That's why I've applied for a nursing program at Southwest. I've got two kids to raise, and I've got to make a living.

Mary Alice Yates
Coal miner
Appalachia, Virginia

> *Poverty is a thief. It steals your dignity, self-esteem, integrity, and even your hopes and dreams—but only if you let it.*

I was raised up one hill, down another, and back in a hollow—way back. We had electricity, but we didn't have indoor plumbing. We had a television, but we didn't have a telephone. I was so poor I didn't have makeup or pretty clothes, and in fact I barely had clothes to wear. I didn't date until I was seventeen, and I was eighteen years old before I had my first kiss. I never brought kids home because I was ashamed of being so poor. Now I feel differently. Even though I'm not particularly proud of how I was raised, I'm not ashamed of it either, because I didn't choose it.

After I graduated from high school, I earned an associate's degree in business management from Bluefield State College, and I began working at Buchannon General Hospital. I started out as an assistant cashier, a few months later I was promoted to assistant credit manager, and a year later I was placed in public relations. After I left the hospital, I worked in the mental health field for two years, but I didn't like the job. I couldn't decide whether or not I should quit, and a friend told me to pray about it; she said if I felt good about staying, stay, and if I felt good about leaving, leave. So I left. I had no idea what I was going to do, but my father-in-law told me I should go into the jewelry business. I thought that sounded like a good idea, and that's when I discovered I was an entrepreneur.

I borrowed fifteen hundred dollars, and I went to a show and bought jewelry. When I came home, I went to people that I knew, and I sold them what I'd bought at the show. I kept expanding, until a few months later I had to borrow more money. Now, three years later, I have my own shop, about forty-five thousand dollars worth of jewelry, eight thousand dollars worth of jewelry-sizing equipment, a security system, a safe, and I own the business free and clear. I'm constantly in awe that my business has done so well, but it isn't very hard to understand. I'm honest and I give my customers good deals. I provide them with a service they like, and they provide me with a living I like. I feel good about what I've accomplished.

I own my own business, my own house, I'm studying to be a gemologist, and I'm happily married. I attribute everything I have, mentally, physically, spiritually, to the Lord, to Jesus Christ, first and foremost. I also realize, however, that I'm an important part of the equation. A lot of people, especially Christians, want to blame everything on either Satan or God, but there's a third person involved, and that's me. We make an awful lot of wrong decisions that the Devil doesn't have anything to do with; we just screw up.

A. Bonita Fletcher
Entrepreneur
Grundy, Virginia

> *When I was a junior in high school I made up my mind*
> *I was going to be a trooper, or I was going to die trying.*

My first duty assignment after the academy was as a road trooper in Harlan County, and I've been here ever since. Even though I graduated with a B.S. in police science, I was real hesitant when I started, because I was the first woman in eastern Kentucky who was doing what had always been a man's job, and I didn't know how people were going to accept me. When I went into restaurants with other troopers, people just stopped and stared, like the E.F. Hutton commercial. But that didn't last long. Everyone here has been extremely nice to me. I was a road trooper for six years before I became a detective.

As a detective, I investigate thefts, burglaries, child abuse cases, and even murders. The ones I hate the most are child abuse cases. It really bothers me when I see a kid abused. I enjoy working the murder cases; they're sad but challenging because you've got more evidence to collect and you have to prepare for a court date. My most interesting case happened last year. Two juveniles from Michigan came here to stay with a friend, and while they were here they beat an elderly widow to death. It was the most severe beating case I'd ever seen. Now we're seeking the death penalty on an eighteen and a sixteen year old. I think we've got an excellent case.

Part of doing the job is dealing with fear. There are times out there when I've been deathly afraid. One night I was with another trooper, and when we pulled up to investigate a complaint about a drunk shooting a gun, fire started coming at us. We crawled underneath the cruiser and tried to make ourselves very little. Another time I chased a drunk into his house, and he pulled a shotgun out and was leveling down on me, but his son grabbed the gun. If he hadn't, I probably would have killed him. He eventually pled guilty to wanton endangerment, DUI, and driving on a revoked license. He apologized in court. He said he was drunk and didn't know what he was doing.

I've also had some funny things happen. Once I arrested a man for drunk driving who'd run his truck into the side of the mountain. When I told him he was under arrest, he looked at me and said, "There's no damn woman going to arrest me." Then he called me a bad name, and I got mad, picked him up, and threw him over the trunk of the cruiser. When I went around to the other side of the car, he was crawling toward the cruiser and said, "Ma'am, where do you want me to sit?"

Alice M. Chaney
Detective
Kentucky Highway Patrol, Post #10
Harlan, Kentucky

A hundred thousand people have already left West Virginia.
If the railroads would lower their prices on coal,
it would start the mines booming again,
and people would come back home.

My father started working for the Aircoma Coal Company in Aircoma, West Virginia, in 1918 or 1920, but I didn't live at home. I lived with my sister. Her husband was a coal miner, and he worked from daylight to dark. When I was fourteen he got his back broken in the mines. He was in a cast from his chest down to his hips. In 1938 I went to work at the dime store to support that family.

Back then, everybody in Logan was poor, and the economy was so bad we struggled just to get by. I worked at the theater, then I worked at a hardware store. I never married or had children. I lived with my sister, and I spent my life working. I saw so much poverty that it made me work towards bettering myself, to keep on going, to make something out of myself. I refused to get down in the gutter, and it paid off. In 1958, I started working as a secretary for the United Mine Workers. Since then my life's gotten much, much better. I think that's the way most people feel who have something, and I think that's the way a lot of coal miners feel. There are a lot of good people who are coal miners.

I would like to see the mines back like they were in the 1960s. That's when things were really booming and people were working. I think we can get back to that if we can just get the nonunion mines to hire from the panel. When miners are out of work, they put them on the panel, based on seniority, but the nonunion mines won't hire from the panel, and that's causing a lot of heartaches. Our insurance is also a real problem.

Back in 1978, when Arnold Miller was president, he signed a contract that let each mine carry its own insurance, and that was a mistake. Whenever a mine shut down, then all the miners who worked there lost their insurance. It didn't used to be that way. When I started working with the United Mine Workers they had the Health and Retirement Fund. All the companies paid royalties into the fund based on how many tons of coal they sold. When they did it that way, the fund paid all the bills, and the miners didn't have to worry about their health insurance.

The downturn in the coal economy has made the county look to other places for jobs. They've tried to attract industry by building better roads. We have better roads than we've ever had, but they're still not that great. Unless they're able to attract some kind of new industry in here, or unless the mines start up again, I would say the majority of the younger people will leave because they'll move wherever they have to in order to find a job.

Martha Cody
Retired secretary
United Mine Workers of America
Logan, West Virginia

> *Once I told Bobby . . . someday we'll have*
> *a mountain of clothes, a mountain of food,*
> *and a molehill of money. And that's what's happened.*

Mother was born and raised in Noah Hollow. She had an old horse named Dan, and after Daddy left, she and her sister, Suitie, used Dan to haul coal from a slate dump; that's how they made their living. They sold a wagon load of coal for two dollars. She also built our two-room house; there were seven of us that lived there. By the time I was five, mother had worked the slate dump out, and she started using a mule to plow gardens. She got twenty-five cents a day. We didn't have enough food to eat, and we didn't have shoes to wear. When I was thirteen I started driving a coal truck, and I drove it until I was twenty-two, when I had my first child.

I married Bobby Simpson when I was twenty. The first house we ever lived in was a two-room chicken coop at one time. Later on we finally ended up back on Cranks Creek. Bobby started losing his sight in 1962. By 1982, when we decided to build the center, Bobby couldn't drive nails on account of his vision. The boys held the boards, and he bolted the first building together. It's still standing today. When we got in a real hard place, I'd work a day for my sister, Lydia Surgender, at her used clothing store. That would buy supper. My heart's always been with poor people. It was then, and it is now.

When we were growing up, we didn't have Christmas every year, so when I started the center, I wanted to have a big Christmas. We started doing it in 1983, and we took care of 250 people. We've done it every year since. In 1985, John Long, a reporter with the *Louisville Courier Journal,* wrote three stories from Thanksgiving to Christmas. We had donations galore, and on December 23rd, twenty-nine hundred people showed up. I was devastated, but, believe it or not, we had food for all of them. Since then, we've been interviewed by the *Lexington Herald Leader, Washington Post,* and *Philadelphia Inquirer.* One year Tom Brokaw did a story on us, and after they left Cranks Creek they went to George Bush's house. I thought that was ironic, because there's a lot of difference between his house and mine. They don't strip-mine around his house.

After they strip-mine, they push all the dirt over the mountain. If you get a hard freeze and a warm rain, it washes off, and that's what happened here. We were devastated by the 1977 floods, but it took a long time to get settlements from the coal companies. The coal companies were ruthless. At that time there weren't any laws to make them put anything back. I went to Washington, D.C., trembling like crazy, and I talked to Stewart Udall, secretary of the interior. As a result of those talks, we got new laws on strip-mining. Now a lot of local people think I'm against coal mining altogether, but that isn't the case. My heart's always gone out to miners. There're monuments in Harlan, one to the wars and one to the men killed in the mines. If you count the names, you can see that we've lost more to the mines than we have to the wars. A lot more have died from black lung.

Rebecca Simpson
Director
Cranks Creek Survival Center
Cranks Creek, Kentucky

> *Even though we were poor, there was a lot of love in our house;*
> *there was always room for one more,*
> *and when we got that one more,*
> *there was still room for one more.*

The reason I started doing community work was because of Sister Bernie Kennedy, a nun from Boston. She runs the St. Mary's Health Wagon now, but she used to have a clothing sales center. One day she asked me to help her sell clothes. She sold clothes for a little bit of nothing; some for a quarter, and some for a dime. But some people couldn't afford anything, so she just gave them what they needed. My heart really went out to those people, and what she did for them inspired me.

I worked with her for several months, and I got used to helping people and giving them something they needed. Some of them needed clothes or information or transportation, so I did whatever I could to help them. I felt good about helping other people, and that's when I started working at the center.

I've been at the center fifteen or sixteen years. But Deacon Binns got the whole thing started. At first we worked in the Church of the People, but then we moved into the big building we're in now, which used to be a grocery co-op before it went under. Now it's the Binns-Counts Community Center.

I'm the preschool coordinator. We work out of the little house next to the big center. We operate four days a week, and the children's parents run the school. While the children are in school, ten or twelve of the parents go to GED and literacy classes. Three of them have already gotten their GED's, and Turner Archer has just passed her assistant nurse's test. Now she's studying to be a registered nurse. Those women are intelligent mothers. They just need a little encouragement, because they're afraid they'll say the wrong thing over the phone or put down the wrong thing on an application. We give them the skills they need to succeed, but that isn't all we do at the center.

During the strike, the women at the center served from two to three thousand men every day, three meals a day; and when we weren't cooking food, we were on the picket lines. I was there when they took over Moss 4. I did whatever I had to do and I felt good about it, because they were trying to take away my father's hospital card.

Economically, things are bad, but hopefully they'll get better. We're incorporated, and two or three factories have come in, but the kids are still leaving. They're going to New York and Boston and Birmingham, just wherever they can find work. Sometimes I sit here and I dream, and I look at things, and I say everything's going to be fantastic. And then sometimes I get depressed and I don't know what's going to happen. I just know if we can't keep the young people at home, the community will die.

Edna Gulley
Preschool coordinator
Binns-Counts Community Center
Clinchco, Virginia

> *I'm glad I can pass on the flag I must soon lay down.*

I started writing for two reasons. First, I loved my father so much I wasn't willing for him to die. I wanted everyone to know what a wonderful person he was. Second, I saw my kids growing up believing all this degrading stuff written about mountain people, and I wanted them to know the truth. But it never entered my mind that my work would be published. I taught myself to type, and I'd just meant to make twenty copies for my grandchildren.

I wanted to tell them that my husband, Willie, was the most intelligent person I'd ever met. He didn't have much education, but he had a bushel of common sense. I married him in 1936, during the Depression. Times were hard, but we had plenty to eat and he always had work. Willie worked in gas, not coal. I don't have a good feeling toward the coal companies. I hated the strip mines because of the environmental damage, and I hated those yellow houses in the coal camps, all bunched together, without any privacy. But mostly I didn't like the coal companies because my family suffered so much from coal. Three of my sisters lost a son in the mines, and one lost two to black lung.

They've written about us like we were starving to death. I remember Daddy said once there were some men going from Harlan County to Floyd County to work in the mines when a storm drove them into our house. We were eating supper at the time, and Daddy said he asked them to sit down and eat. They did, and there was so much food on the table all mother added were seven extra plates. That's how we were starving to death. But you had to work for it. If a man was able to work but didn't, his neighbors left a switch in his door; if he didn't pick up and start doing better, they took him out a few nights later and gave him a good thrashing. But if he was sick and couldn't work, they went in and pulled his corn and brought him a bunch of chickens or a pig. We didn't let anyone starve. One way or another, everyone had something to eat. We took care of our children, the boys and the girls.

I named every one of my children Sarah Ellen before they were born, hoping for a girl, but I never got one. That's why I named the little girl in one of my books Sarah Ellen. Instead, Willie and I raised five boys, and we taught them about Jesus. Three of them turned out to be ministers. By the time they left home, they knew how to cook, how to keep house, and sew. Back then, mountain women were raised to take care of their men, and we did. I petted Willie nearly to death; when he dressed, I was the one that ran the belt through his pants and unbuttoned his shirt off the rack. When he ate, I cut his corn off the cobb and cut his peaches in halves. He was a wonderful man, the most courageous person I ever met. Before he died two years ago, he was accidentally shot, burned in a fire, had heart problems and cancer. He suffered for thirteen years, but he never complained. After he died, things just weren't the same. When you lose someone like that, you're not a whole person anymore.

Verna Mae Slone
Author
Pippa Passes, Kentucky

> *Coal-mining is a life-threatening vocation,*
> *and coal miners deserve every cent of pay*
> *and benefits that they get.*

When I was in sixth grade, Daddy's left leg was broken the first of three different times in mine accidents. After the third accident, the leg wouldn't heal properly; he had to have pins put in to hold the bones together and skin grafts to make it heal. He was in a body cast for several months and that just about caused him to have a nervous breakdown. In the end, his leg shrank, and he had to wear a brace with a built-up shoe and walk on crutches the rest of his life. He wasn't able to go back in the mines. The effect on our family was devastating. When you got hurt, the coal companies were through with you. Their lawyers even tried to keep Daddy from getting his workman's compensation.

After this, there were no extras around our house. I remember one year my mother ordered three sweaters and three skirts for me from a catalog, and I mixed and matched them all winter. One year at Christmas, the man who ran the company store also took up a collection and bought us some groceries with fruit and nuts and candy. He will never know what that meant to me. He brought some joy into our Christmas that year. I met him several years ago and his family and mine are good friends. Sometimes he dresses up like Santa Claus for the children, but to me, he doesn't need a costume. He will always remind me of what Santa Claus means. My sister also helped; when she was in high school, she started working at a drive-in and she saved her money and bought a bicycle for me. I was so excited! Even in times of trouble, God always found ways to bless me.

By the time I reached high school, Dad got his disability from Social Security, which made things a little easier. However, a few years later he started having heart problems. He had no insurance or hospitalization to cover the cost of the heart surgery that he needed. My mother found out that Social Security had a special fund for people like Daddy, and they paid for his open heart surgery. He survived, but there he was, a man in his early fifties, and because of unsafe conditions in the coal mines, his life had totally changed; his legs had been taken away, his good health was gone, he couldn't work, and he couldn't do the things with his friends and family that he used to do. As I got older, I felt that my father and his family had been cheated out of the life that should have been.

After I began working for the United Mine Workers, I became aware of the negative attitude some people have toward coal miners, and it disturbed me very much. I believe the biggest misconception that people have is that coal miners want a free ride. Many people see their contract strikes as an arrogant demand for excessive pay and benefits instead of what it really is, a demand for respect. People who don't like unions should always remember that there would not have been any need for them if employers had treated their employees like human beings, instead of like beasts in the field.

Linda Dare Waugh
Secretary
United Mine Workers of America
Logan, West Virginia

> *Growing up in Grundy*
> *during the sixties and seventies was great.*

My dad was a coal miner, and we lived close to the mines where he worked. When my girlfriend and I went to the post office, we'd stop at the company store and get snacks. On the way home we'd sit by the side of the road and have a picnic. I went to ballgames, to school, stayed all night with friends, and watched television. I grew up with *Lassie, Leave It to Beaver,* and *Bonanza.* I also went to the movies at the old Lynwood Theater, which was absolutely wonderful.

In high school I was a cheerleader for the Grundy Golden Wave. When I was a sophomore my parents bought me a new car, and since I only had a learner's permit, my neighbor rode with me to school and stayed late for cheerleading practice with me so I could drive. The football team was terrible that year. It was also the year the Vietnam War ended. I remember going to a funeral for a boy my parents knew. He was killed in an explosion, and he was lying under the glass in his uniform. It was heartbreaking.

I graduated in 1974, and a lot of my friends went to Pikeville College, but I got married and my husband didn't want me to go. It was one of those macho things. I'm not complaining, because I've settled into a situation where I feel very content. The kind of life I lead isn't for everyone, because some people are very career-minded, but I've always been a homebody. I work at the library three days a week, and I occasionally go shopping in Richmond or Roanoke. I also spend a great deal of time with my dog, Katie. Mostly I enjoy staying at home with my husband, Joe, and my daughter, Leigh Ann.

Leigh Ann is in her first year of college. She's a very mature, together young lady. She was accepted at Radford and was really happy to be going away, but since she was an only child we just couldn't deal with it. We pleaded with her to go to a local community college for at least a year, and she finally agreed, but only after she got a later curfew, a bigger allowance, and a new car.

The Grundy I grew up in isn't a lot different from other parts of the United States. The automobile as a status symbol has certainly risen in the world, even here in Grundy. Another big difference is how regularly we attend church. I was raised in the Church of Christ, and I attended regularly. I'm still God-fearing and God-loving, but I don't attend church regularly. When I do go it's usually to the Baptist church for revivals.

I feel the same way I did when I was growing up, that Grundy is a safe, peaceful, and friendly place to live.

Patsy K. Lockhart
Housewife
Grundy, Virginia

I was born in 1905, and I've seen it all in McDowell County! I was raised in Wilco Bottom, when there were still Indians in this area. I had five brothers and two sisters, and we were brought up by parents who were very strict. My mother was sensitive to the actions of her children. If we had any trouble in school, she said we were disgracing our Momma and Poppa. So she was very strict on us. She made us revere all our neighbors. We had to go to Sunday school and we had to go to church. And we didn't make any noise while we were there either. We weren't allowed to use bad language, and we had to go to school and keep ourselves in school. And it wasn't always easy.

Every day on my way home from school, the boys, white boys and black boys, chucked rocks at me. I don't know why they threw them, just because I was a little girl coming up the creek, I guess. But I'd run and run, and if I made it to Dr. Whitley's office where Momma worked for Dr. Whitley's wife, I was safe. Mrs. Whitley finally got tired of watching those boys throw rocks at me, and she sent me to Harper's Ferry, to Storer College, which was a school for black children. After I came back from Storer, I went to Bluefield State College, New York University, and the University of Pittsburgh, where I got my master's degree in reading. I taught all over McDowell County, and when Mr. John David Bryson was superintendent of schools, he appointed me reading supervisor of all the schools in the county, black and white.

I traveled around the county and observed the teachers' procedures and methods. If they needed help, I helped them. I taught a lot of children how to read, but I think some of the teachers today don't understand how to help children learn to read. You've got to be patient, and you've got to be kind and loving toward children, not hollering and yelling at them. You tell them what you want them to do, then you walk around the room, see how they're doing, and if they're having trouble, you take their little hand and show them how to hold a pencil or show them how to use the chalk. I think teaching methods have gone downhill. There's too much yelling and not enough teaching.

I also think we need to go back to some of the old practices we used to have that made for finer people and more useful citizens. We need to start with the youngsters. The things they do they learn from adults. Once I tiptoed to the back of the room where some boys were supposed to be reading. They were playing cards. I asked them, "Where'd you learn that?" and one of them said, "From my Daddy." You can't fuss with them when that happens. You have to show them you don't do that at school. At school, we learn to read, write, spell, and do our arithmetic. You have to have a quiet voice, sit down with them, and show them that you care about them. If children think you care about them, they'll do anything you want them to do.

Frances J. Long
Retired reading supervisor
McDowell County Public Schools
Welch, West Virginia

The Sandy River District Action Corporation was founded in 1987 to get a statue built to honor McDowell County's coal miners. About twelve of us worked really hard. Two of the older ones have passed away. I'm about the only active one left. We knocked on doors, went to meetings, and talked to hundreds of coal miners. Our first idea was to have a coal miner made out of coal, which seems a little ridiculous now, but that stuck in my mind. We kept going to meetings and we kept talking about it until we decided we wanted a bronze statue, but we didn't even know a sculptor.

We invited sculptor James Bailey from Mercer County to one of our meetings, and he brought some of his work. We liked it, so we decided to let him do the sculpting, but it was going to cost twenty-two thousand dollars. Then there was the cost of the base. At first we thought we'd put it on a concrete base, with the names on metal, but we decided it would look nicer if we set it on granite. I went to North Carolina and chose a twelve-ton piece of solid granite that cost over ten thousand dollars. After that, we had to figure out a way to pay for it.

Somebody suggested that if a coal miner had worked ten years or longer in the mines they could have their name put on the base. We charged one hundred dollars to put a coal miner's name on the monument, and we got names and money from twenty-three different states. Dads came before husbands. If it was a woman, she had her daddy's name put on it before her husband. We dedicated the monument July 4, 1992. Since then it has been the most photographed site in McDowell County, West Virginia. It brings visitors from all over the United States to Bradshaw.

The women really moved this project along. Men will do things if you wait long enough, but women want to get done right now. Men table too many things. They take up too many things for the next meeting. Women say, "Let's sit down and work it out now." Women are better at meetings; they're more apt to sit down and work at things and try to see both sides of an issue. I don't think they come to the meeting with a preconceived idea of how it has to be. There might be twenty-five ways of getting to the same point, and they're more likely to try different ways.

Our group is dormant now, but we still have some work to do this summer. We need to have some dirt removed, we need a wall built in front of the monument, and we need to collect money for general maintenance. Other monuments have fallen into disrepair, and we don't want that to happen to our statue.

Geneva M. Steele
Activist
Paynesville, West Virginia

I'm a roofbolter. That's the most dangerous job in the mine, but I can't spend all day thinking about it, or it will drive me batty. The shaft at VP no. 6 is 1,563 feet deep, and there are places where there are 3,000 feet of rock above my head. I'm constantly advancing into the unknown; that's part of the challenge, a big part. I'm kind of like the first man who stepped on the moon; I'm walking where no man has walked before. It's something to be underground.

My first day underground was August 6, 1979, at Island Creek's VP no. 4 mine. I started as a general inside laborer with three other women. For the first forty-five days we were all red hats, new miners, so they couldn't leave us by ourselves. Our supervisor gave us every dirty job he could find, but none of us quit.

The first job title I ever held was miner's helper. I had to keep the miner's cable out of the road and shovel the ribs in behind the miner while the buggies were gone. Since then, I've done everything they've got to do in that mine; I've been general inside labor, miner's helper, scoop operator, belt shoveler, and roofbolter. Because my job's so dangerous, I've always got to keep my mind on what I'm doing; I can't be daydreaming. I have to constantly observe what's going on around me. The main thing I'm thinking about is staying alive. The company cares more about their equipment than they do their people.

Once I had a big battle with the company over a piece of equipment. I was pinning top with a double head galis, and it was worn completely out. Every time I put the inside jack on the ground, it kicked in and threw the machine up in the air, and it either slapped it against the top or threw it over into the rib. The company wouldn't fix it, so I called the federal inspector. He refused to pull the machine, and I was forced to operate it anyway. I was so upset I had to see a psychiatrist; it just about gave me a nervous breakdown. Several days later it fell over and injured a man's leg. They pulled the machine out then and haven't used it since. It's a shame somebody had to get hurt before they did something. We've learned to depend on ourselves.

We formed the Coal Employment Project to help women get their jobs, because when they first started, it was a real battle. There are four regions: Southern Appalachian, Northern Appalachian, Midwest, and Western. Now we've got members in Great Britain, Australia, and Germany. We're an outreach organization, and over two thousand people get our newsletter. The things that are happening here are happening all over the world. Big corporations want to do away with unionized mines, then go to places like Columbia and Indonesia where they can work people for nothing, ignore safety standards, and kill them off by the thousands.

Linda Lester
Coal miner
Appalachia, Virginia

PART FOUR

WOMEN OF CHANGE

Edith Crabtree says, "Women and children live in the coalfields, too." Yes, and women breathed the coal dust, lived with death, disasters, and disabling injuries, cared for the sick and disabled, joined the thousands of other women in the 1970s to work underground, participated in union strikes, were beaten, jailed, and killed. They lived in coal camps in which their daily lives were controlled by the company; they baked bread, fed children, struggled to keep their clotheslines clean, and they wrote songs about the mines, union struggles, and life in the camps. Some of them lived in very rural, isolated places, and overcame tremendous hardships with hard work and good humor. Many cared for and nursed not only their own children but helped neighbors raise theirs as well.

Three generations of women in the coalfields are represented by these faces and stories. They tell of their efforts to improve a community, build a strong union, thwart environmental damage, enrich the lives of children, gain rights for the disabled, build pride in being Appalachian, and prevent abuse of women and children. Some of the older women were healers, midwives, and farmers, while more recently their daughters organized clinics, developed libraries and programs in the schools, or became community organizers and economic developers. They represent the multicultural heritage of the region. They are not all white Scotch-Irish but represent the great diversity of people who came to the area, including Native Americans who remained in the mountains and African Americans and Italians who came to build railroads and mine the coal. Their experiences also vary depending on their relationship to the industrialization of the region. Some remained in the rural hollows and were more self-sufficient and sometimes impoverished, while others became part of the modern coal towns and dependent on the wages from the industry.

Unfortunately, the history of women's role in the coalfields and their struggles to improve family life and communities has been poorly documented, partly because much of their work is conserving, preserving, trying to hold the family and community together and survive the onslaught of industrialization and exploitation. These tasks are usually not documented. Women telling their own stories is one way to restore that history. They also have to fight against other images of mountain women: the dumb hillbillies such as Daisy Mae or Mammy Yokum or the pitiful, pathetic mountain woman with her drunken, moonshine-making husband.

Like women throughout the economy, women in the mountains have been used as a reserve army of labor to be mobilized in time of need, such as Rosie the Riveter in World War II. Many women left the mountains for work but returned when plants closed or when they were called back home to care for parents and other family. They have been marginal to the economy and used also in the more monotonous, menial, lowest paying jobs. In the coalfields there were few jobs open to women, so it was a big deal when women were able to enter the mines and work for "grown-up wages." Even there they had to prove themselves over and over and survive harassment.

Some of the women are "outlanders" who came to the mountains not as land buyers or developers but as missionaries, teachers, nurses, helpers, and healers. Many of these became adopted daughters of the mountains, were evangelized by the landscape and have been able to bring needed skills and a vision of alternatives that helped ameliorate some of the abuses of the system. They could also take risks that local women were unable to do. These outside women were often aggressive, restless, unconventional people who found work in the mountains adventurous.

Women have been leaders in all the movements for social justice in the coalfields. They have worked for better living conditions for their families, health care, black lung compensation, pensions, and safe and healthy communities. They have developed schools and social services and worked to make bureaucracies respond to the needs of their families and communities. Looking over their shoulders is a host of witnesses from the past including Granny Hager, Sara Ogan Gunning, Widow Combs, Alice Lloyd, Bessie Smith, and Mother Jones, for these women are part of a long tradition of strong women who have been very important in the history of the region.

As the economy is rapidly changing in the coalfields, as people are beginning to understand what the area might be like without coal being the main source of employment and the dominant force in the community, there is both joy and terror. For some there is a sense of relief and freedom. For the first time they are not controlled, not dependent; they can make some choices, do things themselves with what little is left. Women are playing a most important role in developing a new economy and rebuilding deserted and devastated communities. They are the leaders in economic development activities, seeking a more humane, just, and equitable economic system for the coalfields, one no longer fully dependent on coal.

Women today are trying to develop a new economic model of community-based development that emphasizes livelihood, an economy that is not exploitive of people and resources but sustainable and self-renewing. The infrastructure that they emphasize is education, where people grow and develop along with the economy. They work to rebuild communities, the civic infrastructure of relationships and responsibilities to each other. Women in their development activities encourage and promote creativity, seek to protect cultural traditions, and emphasize preserving, nurturing, and conserving. Women have always been the ones to "make do," recycling in quilting or using leftovers in the soup pot. They tend to the soil and water to feed the family. In the organizations they create they encourage more democratic participation with less hierarchy and dominance. Coalfield and mountain women today seem to be trying to understand the new world economic system, trying to rebuild community in a global setting, but also, as in the past, sharing a concern for the safety and future of loved ones, a trust in the value of family and community, the courage to fight against injustice, and a belief that people working together can make a difference.

Helen M. Lewis
New Market, Tennessee

> *When we hear someone at the door,*
> *we never turn them away, because it may be Christ knocking.*

The Catholic presence here goes back to the 1940s. The church itself was built in 1954, and we started the Holy Trinity School in 1957, in the basement of the church. They taught grades one through eight in one room. One teacher taught grades one through four on one side of the room, and another teacher taught grades five through eight on the other side. This house was a miner's house that was originally on the other side of the road. They moved it over here, covered it with brick, closed in the front porch, and turned it into a convent.

When we first started coming here, in the mid-1960s, it was a real culture shock. We knew there was such a place as the Appalachian Mountains, but we never dreamed we'd be here. What surprised us back then was what the people down here didn't have and didn't expect to have. In the city, we had running water, and decent heating and good clothes. Down here, the people used well water, heated with potbellied stoves, and dressed in rummage. Although there were some cars, a lot of people didn't have one; they walked wherever they went. So many people lived in shacks up in the mountains, and their kids walked to school barefoot. Most of them didn't have a telephone, and many of our children's parents couldn't read or write.

When we came back in 1990, we saw great improvement. I can see how people coming down for the first time would see it differently, but since some of us had the advantage of seeing it in steps, over a twenty-year period, there has been a great improvement. But more still needs to be done. There are more and more people who value education, and they continue to encourage the kids, and I think all our parents can read and write now. And the housing situation has improved tremendously. That was a big handicap. Gains have been made. And now not all of our children are poor. Many of our children come from wealthy families, but the poor are still with us.

One of the things that continues to amaze us is the powerlessness of the poor. If you don't help them, they don't have too many resources to help themselves. I know one family with nine children, and they have no income except food stamps. When the mother doesn't have money for electricity, they cut it off. The next week, they cut her water off. Can you imagine nine children, the oldest one ten, with no water and no electricity? I know an injured miner who waited five years for a settlement. Another man I know worked for the city, and he got hit in the back of the head with a backhoe. He's permanently brain-damaged, and they still haven't settled with him. They make them wait, hoping they'll settle for less. It's disgraceful.

Sister Mary Sebastian
Sister Mary Roberto
Sister Mary Claire
Sister Janet Marie
Holy Trinity Convent
Harlan, Kentucky

> *Things have changed a lot, and it's not for the better,*
> *it's for the worse.*

I was raised during the 1920s. I had seven brothers and six sisters. My father was an engineer, and my mother was a housewife. She worked in the garden and took care of the cornfields. We raised a lot of corn back then. We lived on the road in the mountains, and we played in the woods. Everybody had horses, cows, hogs, and chickens. We raised everything we ate, and we had plenty to eat. We only went to the store to get flour, coffee, and sugar. The thirties were hard years. Nobody had much except what they had to eat. We put big gardens out in the bottoms. We canned beans, corn, just about everything. When we were all at home we used half-gallon jars. That fed everybody, along with a whole big pan of biscuits. We got electricity in 1948; before that we cooked on coal or wood stoves.

I was twenty-two when I got married. Courting was a lot different back then; we'd go to church or sit around the house, and the boys came to see us. I'm a Baptist and we went to the Old Regular Baptist Church about a mile above the house. Every Saturday night Cecil came around and sat on the porch. Dad never said anything. He wasn't too bad. After Cecil and I got married, we stayed with his grandpa for a year and a half, then we moved to my mother's and built a little two-room house. We stayed in that house until 1945, then we built another house with six rooms. It was good enough. He had work to do all the time. Until he started carpentering, he worked in the mines. I worried about him when he was in the mines, but he never got hurt.

Cecil and I had four children. I had a midwife when I had the children. There weren't any doctors. People used pennyroyal and dog fennel to make tea. My grandpa drank ginger tea every night. He lived to be a hundred. It must have been good for him. I never had the whooping cough or measles until after I got married. I survived both of them. I was pretty sick with the measles. More people died in the 1918 flu epidemic than died in the war.

I don't think there's much future for Buchannon County. It's all mined out, and it ain't doing no good at all. I can't tell you how people are going to get by, because I don't know. They started cutting timber first, then they went to mining, and now they're back to cutting timber. I guess that's all there'll be if they don't find something else. It's not like it was when I was growing up, everyone helping everyone else. I don't know what's got into these young kids. They're not helpful at all. The Devil's got in them, I guess.

Lula K. Davis
Mountain woman
Hurley, Virginia

> *It's been a good life, but if I had it to do over,*
> *I'd have stayed in school and gotten an education.*

I made straight A's in school, but I had to quit when I was in third grade to help at home. I was one of ten children. I married Estel Reynolds when I was fifteen. Estel helped his daddy farm, but after we got married he went to work in the coal mines at Swords Creek. I worked at Honaker in the shirt factory sewing on pockets. We had three children, but when I was twenty-five Estel got sick. He had a bad heart, and I decided if I was going to work I might as well work in the mines where I could make some money.

I started as general inside labor, rock dusting, at Island Creek's VP no. 2. I was a red hat for ninety days, then they put me on a belt drive. It wasn't long until we had a layoff. After the layoff, they hired me at VP no. 6 as general inside labor shoveling the belt, and I did that until I signed for a supply motor job. Later on I bid on a belt drive job and got it. I've done that job ever since. I've worked in the mines seventeen years, and most of the men have been pretty good except for a few knotheads.

Once we kicked an old boy out of the bus over his old dirty mouth. We'd already told him what we were going to do if he crawled into that end of the bus when the shift was over. Sure enough, when the shift ended he crawled back in there with all the women and started running his old dirty mouth. When he did, we turned sideways and kicked him out of the bus while it was still running. "Wait a minute," the boss said. "Ralph Ward fell out of the bus."

The only other time I had a problem was at Island Creek no. 2. The second day I was there, I was still wearing my red hat and I wasn't allowed to work the face with the rest of the miners, so the boss let me sit down where he could see me. One of the men kept sitting down next to me and putting his hands on my shoulders. I told him several times to stop, but when he didn't, the next time he put his arm around my neck I hauled off and slapped the fire out of him. "I heard that plumb up into the face," the boss said. "If he bothers you again, I'll give you my hammer." I yelled back, "I don't need your hammer!" He never put his hands on me again.

My husband had a heart attack and died last October. He was fifty-five. It's been awful tough on me. I go to the Harmony Church in Belfast and the people have been real good, but it's the roughest time I've ever been through. I've been under a doctor's care since then, but it's awful lonesome at the house. I hope they'll let me go back to work pretty soon. I want to get back with my friends at the mine. I don't know if I'll have the same job, but they'll find something for me to do for another two or three years until I retire when I'm fifty-five.

**Opal Reynolds
Coal miner
Swords Creek, Virginia**

> *I was with Lewis for fifty-two years. We thought we were young.*
> *He died in July 1993 and we still thought we were young.*

When I go out, I tell people I'm Bertha Lacy, and I'm respected. So are my children. I don't think you know what life is all about unless you have children, and I ask the Lord daily to keep and bless them. When I call, they're there. It makes me feel good. I didn't have sisters and brothers or aunts and uncles, but I've had eleven children, three miscarriages, sixteen grandchildren, and seven great-grandchildren. I've been blessed.

I graduated in the upper group at Kimball High School in 1934. I lived in Hemphill at the time, and in order to get to school, I rode the bus ten miles. When we got there, if the road was slick we walked up that hill. Sometimes we pushed the bus up the hill. The school's gone, but I'm fighting to get a monument where the school was so when cars drive by on Highway 52, their lights will hit it, and it will shine, so they can see the spirit of Kimball High School still lives!

After high school I got married, but my first husband was a drinking man, and he died from tuberculosis. I asked the Lord to send me a better man the second time, and he did. He sent Lewis Lacy. He was a deacon in the church, and he didn't smoke or drink. He came here off the farm in Virginia on Sunday and went to work for the railroad on Monday. It was the only job he ever had. He was a track walker. He walked track checking bolts to see if they were out of line. He worked all the time. Sometimes he'd work two or three days without sleep. Then he'd sleep a little bit and go back to work again. Seven days a week. He walked three hours on Saturday and Sunday. We had eleven children, and we all worked.

Mostly we worked to buy Christmas presents for each other. The children sold the *Welch Daily News,* the Bluefield Sunday paper, and *Grit* magazine, and I made aprons and sold them for a dollar or two. We belonged to the Christmas club, and we put a dollar in every week. Anything we made above a dollar we kept in a jar and saved for vacations. Lewis had a pass on the N&W Railroad, and the whole family rode the train for free. We went to Farmville, Virginia, to see my mother-in-law and to Virginia Beach and Cincinnati, just anywhere we wanted to go.

During World War II they gave out ration tickets for clothes, food, and shoes, and I signed people up for ration tickets. We raised our own meat, hogs, and chickens, and sometimes we'd put up five hundred jars of food from the garden. Lard was rationed, but we made our own so I gave my share away to help people out.

In 1964, my children were the first black kids to go to Welch High School. The bus to Kimball High School didn't run by our house, so I called Mr. Bryson and asked him what he was going to do. He said, "Mrs. Lacy, you put them on any bus you see." I said, "They don't have one going to Kimball High." He said, "Is there one going to Welch High?" And I said, "Yes sir." And he said, "Put 'em on it."

Bertha Lacy
Housewife
Roderfield, West Virginia

*I want to help people who are between the cracks;
they might need transportation or food or clothes
or maybe even just a ride.*

Things have sure changed. When I was growing up the mines were running, and they worked a lot of men. We had a community school, two theaters, and dances. We used to ride our bikes up and down the streets to the old school building, but now with all the coal trucks it's dangerous for kids to be on the road. There's nothing for the kids to do in the area. It takes them an hour to get to the movie. The only activity within thirty minutes' drive is bowling. The kids are our main concern.

The Big Creek People in Action wanted to create jobs so the kids could stay home. A group of us thought it would be nice to turn the abandoned schoolhouse into a place for our kids. We wanted to keep them off the streets and keep them from getting involved in alcohol. We went in front of the school board with a local minister and asked for the old building. They approved the idea within a couple of months, and we immediately started working on incorporating ourselves as a nonprofit organization.

Now we have the first certified child care center in McDowell County through Concord College. The Public Service District also has a room in the building. They've been working to solve water problems in our area. One group, the Wildcats, sponsors dances for the kids, and we have an exercise program and karate. We also have a GED class. Last year we had sixty-two in class. I've already gotten my GED and my nursing assistant's certificate.

We'd like to create small job developments and entrepreneurships. We have a really good Mountain Music Association, and we want to involve them in a way that creates musical, cultural, and technical jobs for the kids. We have a room upstairs where we could build a recording studio and market the music. We also have several people who make beautiful quilts, and they'd like to start a catalog operation. Some of the women thought about doing a commercial kitchen where they could make chow chow or vinegar and market it under their own label. What we're trying to do is create a cultural, economic, and educational cooperative.

We judge our success by getting people to speak up who haven't spoken up before. Last year, a lot of people stepped up on the front lines, saying they'd had enough, that they wanted something and they were willing to fight for it. It wasn't just one or two people; it was a lot of people. They're stepping up and being counted, and it's had a real impact; people from other places have called and said, "I've heard about what you're doing, and we want to know how to do it in our community." These people come from places that have nothing, but they're willing to work hard to get something.

Linda Underwood
Big Creek People in Action
Caretta, West Virginia

> *I heard the water knocking at the back door, so I opened it up*
> *and let it out the front door, and people hollered,*
> *"Get them kids and run." I said, "I'm not leaving*
> *until the house does," and it never did.*

In 1948, my Dad got killed in a rockfall at the Calvin Mines in Virginia. My mother was a housewife. She spent her time raising kids. She got up at three o'clock in the morning, fixed breakfast, and cleaned house. Usually, we got up and helped her, and ordinarily, by daylight we were in the cornfield. The ones that weren't big enough to use a hoe went in front and pulled weeds, and when we planted, the little ones dropped seeds.

People helped each other out back then. We had big apple peelings and bean stringings. A bunch would gather in and go to one field, then they'd all gather in and go to the next neighbor's, until they got them all hoed out. That's the way we'd do when we picked beans and corn and had apple butter stir-offs. On Sunday, we had church at each others' houses. After church we'd stay all day and eat dinner and supper. Most of the preachers were Baptists.

I left home when I was sixteen. I was kind of thrilled about getting married and moving out and starting a family of my own. Jack Baldwin and I had five children. I had a doctor with my first one, but when the second baby came, the doctor almost killed me and the baby. He wasn't any kind of a doctor. He killed I don't know how many babies. Anybody who came along at Clover Split Camp and said he was a doctor, the coal company would hire him, whether he had a license or not. I had to go to the hospital to save my life and my baby's life. When the rest of my children were born, I made them get a midwife because I didn't trust doctors anymore.

And I learned not to trust the weather. Once I heard an awful racket, and when I looked up water was coming in the doors and windows. People hollered at me to get the kids and run, but I told them I wasn't about to get my kids out there and get them drowned. They said, "You're going to get washed off." And I looked at them and laughed. I stayed right there, and after it was over, we were all right, but I had a mess to clean up. People said it was a cloudburst, but I think all the logs and trees in the holler burst loose and came out.

It's been a hard life, but it's been a pleasant life. I was a lot happier when my husband was living. My husband had a bad heart; it was caused by the dust that settled in his lungs. He died one night in his sleep. Dying don't scare me a bit. God put all of us here to take us one day, and when he gets ready for me, I'll be gone. There's no sense worrying about it. The one thing none of us can shun is death.

**Pauline Baldwin
Mountain woman
Le Junior, Kentucky**

My grandmother Musick had a big influence on my life. She loved books and reading, and I spent a lot of time with her. I grew up with tales of Brer Rabbit and Beatrice Potter's Squirrel Nutkin and all the other different storybook characters. At an early age I learned to love books the same way she did, because I learned from her what a wonderful realm of fantasy, literature, and storytelling was out there. I think what was planted early in my mind by her almost had to come full circle back to me, to the point that, when I was offered the opportunity to work in a library, I left teaching for books. I had to go back to earn a master's degree in library science, but it was what I'd always wanted to do. I have tried to use knowledge and books to help destroy stereotypes of Appalachian people.

I first became aware of stereotypes several years ago, when I was teaching English at Grundy High School. As I took my students on trips around the state, they were often labeled as mountain people or rednecks or hillbillies and when you're trying to build a positive self-image in teenagers preconceived notions like those make my job a lot more difficult, almost impossible. Kids need positive self-esteem to succeed. I took trips to England and Scotland with my students and I saw what a tremendous sense of self-confidence they got when they had been out in the world and survived, which is something we all need.

We're competing in the global community, and I see accessibility to information as a way to tie Appalachia into what is going on in that community. The real danger is that we don't want to lose our sense of Appalachian culture, which is characterized by an attachment to the land and the attachment our people feel toward one another. If there is a way to hold on to who we are and our sense of community and our sense of attachment to the mountains and the land and the culture, we want to retain that, but I guess like a lot of other minorities we've got to figure out a way to balance who we are with what we want to be.

I like to think information technology is the answer; computers and networks and fiber optics are going to make Appalachia accessible to the world, so I'm fighting hard to get the library the same information technology everyone else has. We now have a connection to the Internet. We borrow and loan books throughout the southeastern United States. The turnover time is sometimes just a couple of days. We'll soon have sources for full text periodicals on-line. In a sense, we'll be hooked up to the world.

Patricia Musick Hatfield
Director
Buchanan County Public Library
Grundy, Virginia

You can't just solve one problem. . . .
You always have to fight other battles,
regardless of when they arrive.

In 1964, the Council of Southern Mountains sent a representative to talk to the political and social leaders in McDowell County. The most important idea that came out of their discussions was that in order to break the cycle of poverty, they had to start working with children when they were very young. The McDowell County chapter of the Council of Southern Mountains was formed and applied to the Ford Foundation for a grant to train thirty-two women to work with young children in child development centers. They started a six-week training program in February 1965, and sometime about midway through their training, those thirty-two women became the nucleus for the Head Start program in McDowell County.

Now we have 405 children in twenty-two classrooms, served by a staff of ninety-five people—cooks, drivers, teachers, assistant teachers, and social workers. We've worked hard to reduce the ratio of children to adults and to create individualized learning plans for children. There's been a real big emphasis on getting the children's health needs corrected, particularly dental problems. Over the years, a lot of our children who otherwise wouldn't have had an opportunity to do so have gone on to become doctors and lawyers and teachers, but we still have problems with teen pregnancies, child abuse, alcohol, and drug abuse. We've learned we can't just focus on children. We also have to focus on creating a strong infrastructure.

After the coal companies left, the water system was sold to a private owner, and he allowed it to deteriorate to nothing. At my house, I haven't drunk the water or cooked with it for six years. People didn't think we could ever change the situation, but three years ago the Public Service District was formed and in two weeks we're going to turn on clean water in Coalwood and Caretta. We've got state-of-the-art plants, and in Coalwood we're developing a sewer system that will create wetlands; that's not totally funded yet, but we think it's going to be because the state just asked us to condense our ten-year plan to two and a half years. We're also looking at economic development.

We've worked very hard to become one of President Clinton's Economic Empowerment Zones, or an economic community. We'll use the money to make Coalwood and Caretta model rural communities and to solve our problems, the same ones communities have everywhere else. The drug culture has really impacted families here. We're trying to help young men and women with Youth Fair Chance, an employment program for people up to age thirty who dropped out of high school or who have been sidetracked by drugs or alcohol. I see some real positive things happening in McDowell County.

Helen K. Carson
Retired director
McDowell County Head Start
Coalwood, West Virginia

> *When something needs fixing at my house, I fix it.*
> *When something needs fixing in my county, I fix it, too.*

When I started, I wasn't given a job description, just the key to the front door, two desks, and a can of pencils. Since our only other natural resource in McDowell County besides coal is timber, I wrote letters to all the major furniture manufacturers in the country and tried to get them to come here. I even paid my own way to Sweden to talk to furniture makers there. Some of them were interested, but when industries came here and saw that we had no sewage and that the roads were in bad condition, they didn't see us as a profitable venture.

That's when we decided to quit chasing smokestacks and start thinking in terms of sustainable development. We decided if we could start one business, with people inside the county that had a stake in it because they lived here, then we'd have sustainable development. I'm not the only one that saw it that way. Marshall University did two studies, and they said we needed a change in attitude. Our attitude was, "It's a depressed town, nobody's ever going to help us, and nothing's ever going to get done." When we looked at that attitude, we discovered it existed partly because everyone all over the county was operating in isolation from everyone else. That's when I decided we needed to unite the county and act as one people with one voice, and by doing that we could give people a sense of self-pride; not only would it change their attitude, it would also be a major economic achievement.

Through a mini-grant program funded by the Benedum Foundation, we've started ten community groups that have done marvelous things for their communities. It's all dependent on grass-roots organization. Sometimes we have three hundred people at workshops, and we teach them what rights they have and what choices they have and that they can control their own destinies. The training we've provided is unifying people and getting them to believe in themselves. Through this process, the county's beginning to act as one unit rather than as a group of isolated communities, and now we're in a position to go after some major funding. We've even gone to other counties, to show them what we've done, so they can revitalize their counties. As long as the stakeholders have a voice in the decisions, this program will work.

Addie Davis
Retired director
McDowell County Economic
Development Authority
Welch, West Virginia

> *Not one of my children wanted to go to the city to work,*
> *but what are you going to do when there aren't any jobs?*

My daddy's name was Tony Brundymanti. He came to the United States from northern Italy around the turn of the century, and he started working in the Pennsylvania coalfields when he was fourteen. After he served in World War I, he came to West Virginia and went to work at Amonate, where my son works now. He worked at the Newhall mines and he worked at the Caretta mines. He died from silicosis.

I was born at Roderfield, West Virginia, and I grew up during the Depression. We never went hungry. Daddy always had a garden and mother canned two or three hundred cans of food for the winter months. My husband said he went to bed hungry a lot of nights, crying for just a piece of bread. I never experienced that during my time. We even had running water, and my dad always found a way to make a dollar, so we never went hungry. I graduated from Big Creek High School in 1941.

After high school, during World War II, I worked at the Chrysler–De Soto plant in Michigan as a riveter for two and a half years. I made airplane wings. In 1943 my mother got sick, and since I was the oldest girl, she called and asked if I would come home and take care of the children. After she got better, I stayed in War and worked in several department stores. I married William E. Harmon in 1949. I have three children: Steven, Thomas, and Susan. I was a housewife and I raised my children.

From the first day Daddy went into the mines, the union held money out of his paycheck, which now provides for my mother. I'm also getting money because my husband joined the union. If it wasn't for the union, how could I live? I can't live on Social Security alone. My husband was a strong union man. He retired in 1971 and died in 1989 from black lung. My son is a dedicated union man. I saw my role as keeping up the homefront and being very supportive of union activities.

My son still works at Amonate and he says there's work in the mines, but the company says its too expensive and they're just going to close it out. He's been in the mines almost sixteen years. He got a degree from Marshall University in business administration, but he wanted to go into the mines. He liked it. If he gets laid off, at least he's got something to fall back on. I think all my children would have stayed around here if they could have found jobs, like they did years ago, but whether it was economics or politics that caused them to leave, two of them are gone. I wish they could have stayed here. Things sure have changed.

Angelene Harmon
Housewife
War, West Virginia

My grandfather was a juvenile judge and my grandmother ran the Maple Grove Hotel in Lebanon. My father was an electrician and my mother was a housewife. My sister is a chef. I graduated from Lebanon High School, attended Radford College and graduated from East Tennessee State University. I was a schoolteacher for twenty-four years before I went into the mines. I'm the only coal miner in my family.

In 1957, when I got my degree, I decided to move north; I applied for a job in Newcastle County Public Schools in Wilmington, Delaware. I lived in Wilmington for nineteen years. I taught elementary and junior high school physical education and health. For a long time I liked teaching, but I took my work home with me, and I didn't like that. When I decided to move back home, I knew teaching and coal mining were the only two jobs I could get that would pay well. I took a year's leave of absence, moved back home, and on October 30, 1977, I started work at Island Creek's VP no. 2 mine.

My first day underground I swept out A shaft with a broom. Pretty soon I was rock dusting, shooting bottom, taking rock, and pulling cable. The power comes down to one big power box, where a 7,200 volt AC cable runs to another power box and reduces it to 320 DC for the "trolley line"—it's always hot, and it runs the pinner, miner, and shuttle car. The scoop is battery-operated. Since I started I've run a buggy and a scoop, miner helped, and pinner helped, but the job I like best is belt examiner.

I've been a belt examiner at Island Creek's VP no. 6 for the past twelve years. I watch the belt for bad rollers and hot rollers. I can shut down the belt, but I don't like to because there's a lot of responsibility involved in shutting it down. I've only done it twice: Once I found a nest of hot coals and we had to get them out immediately, and once there were eight bad splices that were spilling too much coal. I've always worked the "hoot owl" shift, from twelve to eight, because it works out better at home.

I'll be sixty-two at the end of August, and I'll be retiring. I'm going to help my niece and her husband raise registered quarter horses. I've got a mare in North Carolina getting bred now, and I told my friends at work when she comes home I'm going to hold her hoof until her colt is born. I've not saved any money, but I've got seventeen years in the mines and a partial pension from teaching school in Delaware, so I'll do all right. I worry about the kids; unless they bring in a lot of industry that pays above minimum wage, or unless they get a good technical education in computers and health care, this area will become a ghost town.

Mary Jack Hargis
Coal miner
Lebanon, Virginia

> *I'm a country girl—I never wanted to live in town.*

I was born in 1908, and I was thirty-five before I married. Mother died when she was forty-five, and I promised her I would take care of the children until they were grown. I had three brothers and four sisters, and I stayed at home until all those children left. Then my husband came along, and he was so terribly sweet to me. Oh, he was good to me. I never regretted marrying him. He wasn't just good to me, he was good to everybody. He was a very skillful person, a gifted person. If people had any kind of a breakdown, they'd bring it here, and he wouldn't charge them much to fix it. Sometimes he didn't charge them anything at all. He even made caskets for people. He was a real helpful person. "Get Jimmy Deel!" they'd say. "He'll fix anything."

We lived so far away from doctors, we had to depend on nature to take care of us. When people got sick I gave them herbs. I used to dig ginseng with my mother. It gave us a little money, and people ate it to stay healthy. Another good herb was a little weed called puccoon, or bloodroot. It has a beautiful little white flower, and if you wash it and crush it, it will provide instant relief from a copperhead bite. Comfrey is also very healing. One old lady had a big ulcer on her foot, and we made a poultice from comfrey and healed her leg. A lot of people came for garlic. Garlic's good for just about everything, except sweet breath. But you couldn't cure everything with herbs. Sometimes we needed help, particularly when the babies were born.

Aunt Malvina was the local midwife. She was a little teeny woman, and her little hands were so small, they said if the baby couldn't be born she could reach in and take it with her small hands. The doctor said, "If she can't get the baby, don't you send for me!" She was a wonderful person, and she helped a lot of people. She had a natural way about her, and it just seemed like she could do about anything. She only had to call a doctor once. The afterbirth had grown to the woman's side, and Aunt Malvina was afraid to get it, so she called a doctor. She did things on her own, and so did I. I always tried to take care of my own problems.

If something worried me, I'd go into the mountains and sit by a spring and figure out my problems. Whenever that didn't work, I'd call on the Lord. That's one of the things that's important to me, that God is able to do all things. I was bad off a lot of times, and it didn't look like I could live; my lungs were weak, and I was real sick. Once I had a nervous breakdown, and I had to go stay with my oldest sister. They thought I was going to die, but I didn't. I was a tough old bird. I've had too many prayers answered not to believe in prayer. God can do all things.

Clara K. Deel
Herbalist
Haysi, Virginia

> *When I see the final product at the end*
> *and I know I had something to do with it, it's very rewarding.*

In 1972, my husband and I started the Grundy Little League wrestling program, but we didn't do it by ourselves. Several parents were in the right place at the right time, and we all demonstrated a commitment to our own children, and to the other children in the community. We worked together, and we got things done. We built a gym, provided a Little League wrestling program for the county, and we've won ten state wrestling championships, nine of them in a row.

We traveled everywhere east of the Mississippi looking for tough competition. We competed against schools twice our size so we could learn from them. Our wrestlers weren't always better than the other fellows, but the other guys perceived that they were just because of the dynasty. People in Virginia say that when you put on a Grundy wrestling uniform you're assured of two points when you walk onto the mat. In the world of wrestling, people have heard of the Grundy Golden Wave; however, it wasn't always that way.

In 1971, my husband and his best friend taught at Grundy High School and coached wrestling. Initially they didn't know that much about the sport; they went to the library and checked out a book on the subject. First they practiced on each other, and then they taught the boys. Even though I'd never seen a match, I started keeping score. Later on, I started working the head tables at tournaments, and in 1989 I became the first certified female wrestling official in Virginia. It was hard work, but it was fun because I love children.

I've taught school for two decades, and I think the most important thing about working with children is building their self-esteem. If you can improve their esteem, it's easier for them to learn. Kids who feel good about themselves appreciate what you do for them, and they're willing to accept change. I learned that early in my career. I taught one of the first kindergarten class in Buchanan County, and during that first year my students moved from a two-room wooden building with outdoor toilets to a multimillion-dollar facility.

Since then, I've had a very fulfilling career, but there are still some things I want to do. I want to continue working with children, write a book, earn a Ph.D. in administration and supervision, and continue my work with the Grundy wrestling program. Whatever I do, I want excellence to be the premier feature of my endeavors. I'm a doer, a quiet doer, not a flamboyant one. Although I often take on more responsibility than I should, I always complete the job.

Constance E. Childress
Teacher
Vansant Elementary School
Vansant, Virginia